Growing Up As a Trappist Monk

Nov. 2003.

Dear Bob + Jonne

Growing Up As a Trappist Monk

Father William M. Nolan

Hope you like it!
Love,
Fr. Nolan.

VANTAGE PRESS
New York

Cover design by David Stockwell

FIRST EDITION

Published by Vantage Press, Inc.
516 West 34th Street, New York, New York 10001

Manufactured in the United States of America
ISBN: 0-533-14356-X

Library of Congress Catalog Card No.:2002092299

0 9 8 7 6 5 4 3 2

To my beloved spiritual father, Dom Robert McGann, O.C.S.O.

Contents

Preface

Since the author himself has written a Author's Note to this delightful, and sometimes poignant, autobiographical journey in a Trappist monastery I will call these few lines rather a Preface. It is not a book review, or a critique, or even a footnote. I was in the monastery at Conyers when Father Nolan, who will always be Frater Mary Gabriel to me, came, and I was there when he left. We both heard an authority in the order say that if you are not mature when you enter the monastery you will never become mature in it. Gabriel's sincere and heartfelt narrative gives the lie to that terrible indictment of Trappist life.

The two monks who meant the most to Gabriel, his Abbot, Dom Robert, and Father Ephrem, both entered Gethsemani, the crème de la crème of Trappist life, when as it was said, "they didn't even speak English" (which mattered little in those days of strict silence—wasn't there a brother there who kept silence in seven languages?). Both matured and mellowed into lovable human beings and as Dom Robert was fond of saying, "mirabile dictu," observant Trappist monks.

Thus the title of this work, *Growing Up As a Trappist Monk,* is as intriguing, even beguiling, as it is appropriate. This short story made me laugh and made me cry, two human reactions that were looked upon with horror in those "growing-up" days. Frater Mary Gabriel was a superstar in that popular indoor sport of Trappist monks, held weekly as a rule, called the Chapter of Faults, nicely depicted in this story. Part of the ritual, after the proclamation and the prostration, were the words of the Abbot,

"What is there against our Frater?" Usually, if not always, the reply would be "Frater makes useless signs." There is no doubt that Frater Gabriel was a master of signs, aided and abetted by some competent brothers whom he mentions in the text. After all, "sign making," like the tango, takes a twosome. Always assigned an appropriate and sometimes silly "penance," as I recollect, he remained rather unconverted. "Useless," however, is a very relative term. What was useless for some, mainly the monk who did the proclaiming, was useful for others especially in the context of "growing up in a Trappist monastery."

The readers of this book will probably form a rather motley group, something like a monastic community itself. There will be some, like myself, who can resonate greatly with the narrative. There will be others who will consider it a "useless" piece of writing. And there will be those who are accustomed to reading Thomas Merton, considered the most famous Trappist monk in modern times, who incidentally had his ups and downs in "growing up in a Trappist monastery." These readers just might be "disedified," that famous word in the old Trappist dictionary. Be that as it may, this sharing of sunshine and shadows under very particular and even unique circumstances is like a cup of cool water for anyone trying to survive and flourish in the process of "growing up."

—Abbot Bernard Johnson, O.C.S.O.

Acknowledgments

Thanks to Mrs. James L. Simmons for her generous help in typing this material and offering encouragement.

Thanks to Mrs. John Mosely for her help and for inspiring me to write this story.

Thanks to David Stockwell for the cover design.

Thanks to Ms. Rebecca Horton for the help with photography.

Author's Note

These are memoirs of my seventeen years as a Trappist monk. It is a highly subjective story and lays no claim to objectivity. I write of a time and place that no longer exists. These are memories of the idealistic, impressionable young man I once was. He no longer exists either. An older, more mature man, I now savor the days of joyful hope that were once part of my life. I do not want them to be forgotten. They are enshrined in this book and in the cloister of my innermost self where I cherish them with gratitude. I hope no one will be "scandalized" at this honest, and sometimes blunt, portrayal of monastic life.

Growing Up As a Trappist Monk

I

Matins: Waiting for a New Day

Matins is the prayer chanted by the monks in the dark hours before daybreak. It is also called Vigils because it is a prayer of waiting for a new day.

I saw my mother standing on the loading ramp at the Greyhound bus station that night in her pink and white flowered dress and little black straw hat that she wore to church every Sunday. She had that distant, guilt-inducing look on her face that was an overlay for some great sorrow that had never been put into words. I thought it was a saintly look or else it would have been too painful to bear. She wore that look in her high-school graduation picture as if she already knew that life would always be a disappointment.

We said good-bye without any external sign of emotion, as was usual for my family. I was leaving her, never to return home, not even for her funeral. She had shown me how to pray and it had led to this. I did not feel the sadness of the event because I was young and eager to start my life's journey. I was eighteen years old, in search of God, on the way to join a Trappist monastery in the Deep South. So my departure from my loved ones was somewhat cool and detached, at least externally.

After a sleepless night on the bus, I saw for the first time the pine-needled trees of the Georgia woods, which would soon become so familiar to me. We were pulling into a forlorn looking little town. The small, dumpy bus station had two drinking fountains

1

outside: one for "colored only" and one for "white only." A small, empty, green wooden building across the street was the train station. The town of Conyers was only about thirty miles from Atlanta, but it seemed like a world away from everything.

A muddy little red pickup truck with rusty sides pulled up and a wiry red-faced thin-lipped, little man with a straw hat jumped out and came toward me saying, "You're probably the new recruit for the monastery. They sent me to get you. I'm Quinlan, the farm boss."

"Yes, I am," was my reply.

"Well, put your suitcase in the back. Let's go." I didn't have a chance to give my name. I guessed "new recruit" would suffice.

The orange clay had bled onto the highway due to a bad storm the night before and the sky was still menacing that morning. The ride was bumpy on an unpaved road and we forded a stream where the bridge had washed out. Quinlan told me this was Honey Creek. The monastery was just around the corner. As we crested the hill, I saw across a field some cows and an old cow barn.

"That cow barn is where they used to live. Those wooden barracks are where they live now. They cut down trees, sawed 'em up and nailed 'em together before they was dry, and built that building."

"The monks did that?" I asked in disbelief.

"Yes, with a lot of help. You know, some of them are not too swift with their hands. And they don't know a thing about money or managing a farm. Without me, they'd go broke."

I felt he was a self-important little man who probably criticized the monks all of the time—and that turned out to be true.

When we pulled up to the barrack-like building I jumped out, grabbed my suitcase, and said thanks as Quinlan yelled, "Step in that little white house. Brother Hugh's in there; he's the shoemaker and the gatekeeper. See ya later." *Yes,* I thought to myself, *probably on the farm where I will be inept and worthless.*

Brother Hugh was in his late sixties or so, bald, with a big

A view of the cow barn that the monks occupied as their original monastery when they first came to Georgia.

plastic hearing aid. He had on a hooded brown robe with a blue denim apron over it. I could tell right away that he was a character, plain spoken, abrupt and almost insulting. He said, "Sit down and wait. I'll get one of the brothers to take you over there. I take it you're a postulant?"

"Yes, brother," I said.

"Well, you look rather frail to me. I doubt if you'll make it. Brother Joseph will take you inside."

Brother Joseph was a handsome young man with a Nordic look and a head shaved to the very scalp. He wore a brown robe with a flowing brown cloak that billowed out in the breeze as he walked before me toward the Guesthouse. He showed me to a small bedroom on the second floor with an iron bed, a table, and two straight chairs. He put my suitcase down, paused, looked at me with clear blue eyes and, almost in a whisper, said, "Father Mary will come to see you." I thought, *what a strange name for a man!*

"He's in charge of novices. You will stay here two or three days before you come to the other side." I noticed his faint yellow beard and mustache, which made him look even younger. I wanted to talk with him and he seemed to want to talk to me as he hesitated, but he also seemed a little anxious to leave. Maybe he felt guilty about talking. Anyway, I never got to converse with him verbally, but later we would find ways to have "sign conversations," the primitive way that monks communicated with each other.

There is no such thing as a "vow of silence" in any religious community. However, the Trappist monks at this monastery—and all over the world—observed silence most of the time in order to be more recollected and devoted to prayer and meditation. The sign language was for necessities. I was aware of this. But I knew from reading books about them that I could always speak verbally to the Abbot, my Confessor, and the Novice Master. That gave me comfort and I really wasn't worried about keeping silent. Later I

This pine-board monastery was built by the monks themselves. They lived here for some years while they engaged in
building a permanent monastery built of steel and reinforced
concrete.

found out it was possible to improvise signs and have fun being outrageous, which was strictly against the rules.

I was one month out of high school and had never been away from home overnight. That night I was sad, apprehensive, and tearful. I did not get up with the monks at 2 A.M. for the first prayers of the day (Matins). When I got up at 7 A.M. I went downstairs for breakfast with one or two other guests. It was sparse and not very tasty—homemade monk bread, soggy eggs, and coffee. Besides the guests, there were two or three men there who were "family brothers" (hangers-on who worked around the place, and generally sat around and wasted time). Usually, they were divorced or otherwise injured or disillusioned misfits who were looking for a place to belong.

They began to tell me about the rigors of the other side, i.e., the monastery. First, the monks would X-ray your heart to see if it was in the right place, and then they would make you clean toilets, scrub the floors, kick dirt in your face, etc. I knew that they were teasing me, but I was anxious to get over there to see what really would happen.

I sat in the little bedroom looking out the window. Five or six brown-clad brothers were walking in a line down the red clay road, hoods over their heads, carrying tools over their shoulders and dangling rosary beads in their hands. I thought of the words over the door that led to the monastery, "GOD ALONE." Somehow, the sight of these men epitomized that to me. I thought, *they don't have anything! God Alone. That's what I am seeking.* I longed for that kind of detachment and singleness of heart.

A gentle tap on the door and Father Mary appeared. He wore thick glasses and held his head cocked to the right, looking almost embarrassed or unsure himself. Gently, I said, "Hello," I stood and greeted him, feeling I had to put him at ease. We then sat in two straight chairs opposite each other.

He looked at me and asked, "Why do you want to become a monk?"

Without a pause I said, "I want to become a saint and live every moment seeking God." I could tell that my answer pleased him greatly. He lit up in a big beaming smile. I had said the right thing! We visited for awhile and he left rather self-consciously saying he would come to get me the next afternoon. He then tiptoed out and shut the door without a sound. I got up and roamed around the Guesthouse. Up and down the hall there were lots of pastel drawings of Jesus, Mary, and the Saints; they were pious, but amateurish. I learned later that they were the creations of a Carmelite nun who was the sister of the Prior.

This place where the guests stayed was austere enough with its plain linoleum floors and sparse furnishings. What would the other side be like?

A bell started tolling and I found a door that led to a balcony over the Chapel where the monks were gathering for Vespers (late afternoon prayers). As I looked down, the brown-robed lay brothers with shaved heads, including Brother Joseph, were gathering in the back to pray their Office with their beads. Bowing profoundly and filing in to the stalls along both sides of the walls facing each other were the white-robed choir novices, also with shaved heads, and professed monks, with only a circle of hair around their heads. They began to chant the Divine Office (the praises of God) in soothing and otherworldly sounds called Gregorian Chant.

The entire interior of the Chapel was painted sky blue. There was a giant statue, seven feet or so, of the Blessed Virgin Mary in front of the Chapel over the altar. It looked as though the monks were gathering under her outstretched mantle and I think it was meant to give that impression. Most of these men were young and vigorous looking. They bowed low in reverence at the end of each Psalm. They chanted in Latin, which added to the mystery of it all. God's presence was in this little pine-board Chapel in the backwoods of Georgia. I was in ecstasy. This scene perfectly fit my imaginings of what a monastery would be like.

That evening in the Chapel I cried some more. I wanted to do this. In fact, I felt I *had* to do it. But I was homesick thinking of my mother and my younger sister who, I felt, needed me. I had left her without telling her that I would never be back. The pain had set in.

A few minutes after I returned to my room, there was a soft knock on the door and a small monk appeared. He looked like an old child. He was Father Francis, the Guest Master. He sat down on the bed beside me and stroked me on the back saying, "I know, I know it's hard." I wiped my eyes and thanked him. He said he had been a monk for twenty-five years. He had two brothers who were priests, one in his hometown of Philadelphia and one in Atlanta. He spoke in a very high squeaky voice and bubbles of saliva formed at the side of his mouth as he spoke. There was comfort listening to him tell about his entering the monastery at a very young age. He was so child-like and simple.

At one point he said, "If you thought of everything good that you like to eat and all the pleasant things you enjoy doing—we don't have any of them here. And if you thought of all the unpleasant things you don't like, we have plenty of them here!" I laughed out loud when he said that. He reminded me of a mischievous elf in a monastic habit.

His visit helped. My resolve to do this was absolute, no matter what the sacrifice. You may wonder why a healthy young eighteen-year-old would want to leave everything, including family, to live in poverty and silence for the rest of his life. At that moment, I could not have explained it or understood it either. But now I would explain it this way:

I had been trained by the Sisters of Mercy who taught me about the shortness of life, the joys of heaven, and (graphically) about the pains of hell, along with the three R's. But these ladies were also loving and kind to me. Being impressionable, I became very devout and began to think about becoming a priest. Making this known to the sisters made them even nicer to me, as you might imagine. I had learned early on how to be submissive and sweet as a way of survival. It was partly innate and partly a result of a few beatings by my father when he was drunk, and living with four brothers and four sisters who were pretty assertive.

I always thought of my mother as somewhat of a victim. She was a stepchild in a large family and did the dirty work as a young girl. My father treated her badly, especially when drinking. As early as I can remember, I felt the need to make her happy. I used to watch her praying in church. Her eyes would be closed and there was a beautiful, serene look on her face. I knew she was talking to God.

When my older brother, Gene, was killed in World War II, I felt so sorry for my mother. I wanted to take his place in her life. From the day of his death I tried to make my mother proud, especially with high grades and honors at school. My older sister, Alice, who became a Sister of Mercy, used to read to me about the saints. My favorite was Francis of Assisi. I wanted to be like him: peaceful, holy, and attached to no worldly things. My imagination was peopled with saints and their doings and miracles.

In high school I had read *The Seven Storey Mountain* and *Seeds of Contemplation* by Thomas Merton, written in his first fervor as a Trappist monk. The romantic picture he painted of monastic life made me long for this kind of silence and solitude, immersed in God's love. All of the above had led me to this place on this date in July, 1949.

There was another matter that influenced me. I had some deep-seated guilt, which I will explain later, that made me feel a need for penance and reparation for myself and for the world. The stories of Fatima's call for repentance and possible worldwide disasters fed into my apocalyptic thoughts.

Becoming a monk promised a different world than I had known and I was determined to become one, even if it meant leaving everyone behind—sort of like a death. I thought prayer and self-sacrifice would bring blessings on my family, more than my own physical presence would. Also, I knew how proud my mother would be to have a son who was a Trappist monk and a priest.

The visit from Father Francis had helped me a whole lot and I felt better. Now it was time for night prayer. I stood in the balcony over the Chapel for Compline (the last prayer of the day). After the psalms had been chanted, all the lights were extinguished except the one that shone on the great statue of Our Lady while the monks sang to her a goodnight prayer, "Salve Regina" (Hail, Holy Queen). Rows of brown-robed and white-robed monks filed out in a line and went up before the Abbot who sprinkled them one by one with holy water as they left the Chapel. The guests, family brothers, and I also went downstairs to get blessed.

I got a good look at the Abbot. He was a patriarchal man with bushy white eyebrows, and a chin that jutted out from a firm square jaw. I was self-conscious as I bowed in front of this awesome figure and filed out of the Chapel. He was to become a real father to me as time went by. But that night he overawed me.

Entering In

Father Mary appeared in my room in the early afternoon. I say "appeared" because he walked so quietly that you didn't hear him coming until you saw him. This was the big day, July 18th, when I would enter the enclosure (the Cloister). I was leaving the world behind for good—no more contact with the sin and strife that prevailed out there.

In my naïve innocence I expected everyone here to be holy, kind, and Christ-like and everything to be perfect. I walked behind Father Mary carrying my little cardboard suitcase. We first went to the dormitory. The walls were unpainted and stained around the windows by rain. There were rows of small cubicles with a blue denim curtain over the entrance to each. Father Mary showed me my cell. Inside the cell was a straw mattress and pillow laid on boards, a few big nails on the wall for clothes, nothing else.

There was no heat in the dormitory and certainly no air-conditioning, but there was a window fan somewhere. I could hear it droning. Depositing my suitcase, we headed downstairs to the novitiate Scriptorium. The Scriptorium was a room for reading, writing, and studying. Each novice had a small drawer underneath the built-in benches that surrounded the room on three walls. There were four large tables with stools that had no backs on them and bookcases neatly arranged on one side. A strong, sweet smell pervaded the place—a gardenia blossom in a jar on one of the tables. Somehow this smell was comforting and strangely supernatural.

This room and the outside yard were the only places a novice monk had to read or study. You could never go to your cell during the day; besides, there was no reason to go there except to sleep, which is why you were not allowed to go there. This would be my home for the next two years.

Tiptoeing, Father Mary led me into a small room that was his office. We had been silent so far. He sat me down and began to tell me verbally some basic protocol. "If you wish to speak to me or any superior you say 'Benedicite' and the superior will respond 'Dominus' as a sign that you may speak." (The Latin word Benedicite means "bless," and the word Dominus means "Lord.") Why these words were used at the beginning of every verbal exchange, I do not know. Neither did anyone else. "You will sleep late for the one month that you are a postulant (candidate)." Sleeping late meant getting up at 3 A.M. rather than at 2 A.M. "You will be called 'Frater Postulant' until you take the habit (don the monastic garb) and receive a new name."

Just then there was a knock. A tall, skinny novice with horn-rimmed glasses entered the room looking very solemn. Father Mary said, "This is Frater Matthew. He will be your Guardian Angel the first month you are here. Just follow him around and do everything he does. There are several other postulants. You will meet them later."

Frater Matthew and I looked at each other suspiciously and exited quietly. When we were in the hall, I turned to ask him something but he put his finger over his lips to stop me from speaking. I was amazed. He took me to a large chart on the wall that had rows of words on it. He would point to a word and show me the sign for it. I immediately looked for the word "sick," thinking that if the work in the fields was too much for me I could always sign that I was sick and, thus, be excused.

Frater Matthew would teach me some signs each day. I followed him to Vespers where he kept showing me the place in the huge decorated book of Psalms we were praying from. The book, all in Latin, looked ancient. I stood beside him in the novice stalls. I stood, sat, and bowed whenever he did. I was so excited to be in the Chapel with all of these holy monks! I peeped out of the corner of my eye to see if any seculars were up in the balcony watching us. I was so proud to be there.

After Vespers, we knelt in silent meditation for fifteen minutes. Then the Abbot gave a loud knock, and we all stood up and filed out for supper. Each monk pulled up his hood as we left the Chapel and walked toward the refectory. We stood on the far sides of the bare, mustard-colored tables. Prayers before meals were chanted, and then we went around the tables and sat down. At each place was a cup, wooden fork and spoon, and a steel knife covered with a white napkin. The monks remained covered with their hoods until the Scriptures were read by the Reader of the Week. Then the Abbot touched a small bell, everyone uncovered, looked to each side to see that each neighbor had all the food he was supposed to have. If your neighbor was missing something you could knock on the table with your knife, hold up the knife, and the Monk Servant of the Refectory would come and supply the missing item. You were never allowed to ask for anything for yourself. You just hoped one of your neighbors would notice, especially on

Feast Days when we had ice cream or candy. Often they didn't notice; I learned that on Christmas Day!

Brother Matthew proceeded to break up his bread in his bowl of milk and eat it with a spoon. This nauseated me. I remember thinking, *I'm supposed to do what he does.* My first battle with literalism. I decided it would be all right to dunk my bread one bite at a time. Someone read, in a monotone voice, from a spiritual book in one corner of the room. Reading with too much expression would have been considered attracting attention to yourself; thus, the monotone voice.

After the meal, we washed our spoons and forks in our cups with water from an earthen pitcher, dried them with the napkin, folded the napkin neatly and laid it over the upside-down cup. Oh, yes, and before that we swept all the crumbs into one hand and ate them. All the monks did the exact same thing. We each silently prayed and left the refectory.

I followed Frater Matthew to the Chapel for a brief visit to the Blessed Sacrament and then followed him downstairs to where the toilets were. They were in wooden stalls called "the cabinets." He entered one and I dutifully entered the one next to him. He made a lot of gaseous noises relieving himself. I sat there thinking, *How unlike a holy monk. I never expected this!* Then we marched down the hall to the washroom where long concrete troughs with white enamel bowls and blocks of lye soap lined the wall. We washed our hands and went outside to walk. Frater Matthew turned and signed to me to go away. So, I walked the opposite direction from him feeling a bit rejected, wondering if he was tired of my following him around.

After Compline, the last prayer of the day, we sang the beautiful good night song to Our Lady and I wept quietly. We filed out for bed. It was 8 P.M. on a very hot night as only summer nights in Georgia can be hot.

The straw mattress and pillow were hard as I rolled over and over trying to find a way to get comfortable. Lying there, I became aware that the sights, sounds, and smells of this day were all different; they were plain and austere. There was a monastic smell, not a bad smell, but an aroma (maybe a mixture of homemade wheat bread, lye soap, disinfectant and, of course, holiness—and, I also thought, *sweat*). Definitely not the smell of "the world."

I lay with my rosary beads wrapped around my hand and thought about home, my mother, and tried to pray. I finally dozed off with a jumble of feelings, anxious for the next day to begin.

Frater Matthew reached through the curtain and shook my mattress—at 3 A.M. which was time to pray. I jumped up, put on my clothes and went to the Chapel for Lauds (praises).

After Lauds, the priest monks filed out and went to the sacristy where they vested for Mass. Each went to a cubicle lighted only by two candles. The rest of the Chapel was dark. Each had a novice or junior professed as a server (altar boy). I knelt in the shadows behind Matthew completely in awe at the slow gestures and whispered prayers of the young priest. I thought, *Someday, I will be there at the altar,* and I felt a rush of joy at the thought.

Breakfast at 4 A.M. was a couple of pieces of monk-made whole wheat bread (no butter) and a cup of barley water, nasty tasting stuff that was supposed to substitute for coffee. It was hot and brown, but the resemblance ended there. We prayed silently before and after breakfast (called "mixt" for unknown reasons). Maybe because the bread was "mixed" with the coffee?

At the Chapter meeting following Prime (morning prayers), the Abbot explained a passage from the Holy Rule of Saint Benedict that had just been read out loud. I listened, striving to hear his every word. His words were strong, simple, and down to earth, and his talks got better day by day for years to come. He was a holy man; I could tell right away.

The Novitiate

Now it was time for work. The monks put on blue denim robes with their hooded scapulars and leather belts (cloth belts for novices) around their waists. The novices were sent out to the farm on trucks to work in the vegetable gardens, dig ditches, build fences, and especially to shovel manure, which I soon became quite accustomed to. That first morning I was on a truck with about eight young novices and the professed monk who would be our boss at work. I was examining each novice to see what he looked like and how he acted. On the ride I saw several of them laughing and making signs to each other. A few kept their eyes closed or looked out at the countryside. No one paid any attention to me and I wondered if they noticed a new man was on board.

We unloaded in a cornfield, strapped bags over our shoulders, and started picking corn. As we spread out through the rows of corn, I saw one tow-headed monk throw an ear of corn at another novice, and then begin laughing. Frater Barnabas was only fifteen years old, I later found out, and a real rebel. A monk with a bucket of cold water came around after a couple of hours. I was relieved because I was about to pass out from the heat and an empty stomach, about ready to make the sign "sick!"

Back "home" we prayed again and then had a steel bowl of beans, a steel bowl of soup, and an orange for the main meal at 11:30 A.M. No meat, fish, or eggs were ever served; even the vegetables were not appetizing. One day I felt something crunch in my spinach and I thought it was dirt (being homegrown), and I signed to the monk next to me, "Dirt?" He smiled and signed back, "Bugs." Occasionally, there was some good food. We got a piece of cheese and a bowl of milk twice a week at the evening meal in the summertime, but mostly the meals were bland or repulsive.

The days I have described were all the same. There were twenty young men and two much older men in the novitiate. We had no contact with the professed monks. But we did somehow become friends with each other, fellow pilgrims on a hard road.

Frater Barnabas sought every opportunity to make signs and since I was new, he felt it a charitable act to make signs with me. He told me how hard the life was for him and that he wasn't sure he would stay (all in crude signs and some made-up signs). One morning, after the Night Office during the Grand Silence (when we were not even supposed to make signs) he told me by signs, "Last night I crucified Jesus." I thought I had misunderstood him, but he repeated it emphatically.

I signed, "How did you do that?" Finally, I got the message that he had committed a mortal sin and I guessed what it was. I signed back, "I'm sure Jesus understands." He shook his head sadly, "No." I was thinking sagely to myself, *This kid should not be here at his age.*

Barnabas talked in his sleep and occasionally walked. One night he somehow got up on top of the partitions that divided the dormitory cells; he was walking on the dividers right over the heads of sleeping monks! How he got down, I don't know. Barnabas left the monastery after a few months and eventually became a police officer in Atlanta. He sometimes came back for a visit to the monastery with his young wife to show her off to the monks.

There were two frater postulants who had entered before me; I walked behind them when we went from the Chapel to meals and to other community affairs. One was an intelligent-looking guy with spectacles and a very pleasant face. After he took the habit as Frater Bruno, he constantly carried a ragged copy of the autobiography of the *Little Flower of Jesus* around with him. I guessed he wanted to be the "little flower" of the novitiate. After profession of vows, he suffered a nervous breakdown and was sent away to Iowa for treatment. When the psychologists and psychiatrists got through with him, he was far from a little flower. (More about Bruno later.)

16

The other postulant was only sixteen years old, handsome and athletic looking, very serious but also friendly. He was a strict observer of every detail of the rule and expected everyone else to be the same. I found this out when he started "proclaiming" me frequently at Chapter of Faults. (This was an observance where the monks could accuse each other in public about faults and breaches of the rule.) I hated that.

It seems I was doomed to walk behind two ready-made saints, or at least they had that reputation with Father Mary. Naturally, I was a little resentful, maybe jealous, of them knowing that I was breaking rules daily and didn't feel like a good novice. I sort of looked down on these paragons of virtue whom I could not imitate!

An older novice (about forty or so) named Mark took me under his guidance. He had gray hair, heavy black eyebrows, a chunky build, and was very bossy and worldly wise. He often had a mischievous look in his eyes. One day he pointed to the book called *Usages of the Cistercian Order,* which contains guidelines for how a monk should behave on every occasion, even going to the bathroom, and opening and shutting doors. Apparently that was where Father Mary learned to move around without making any noise.

Pointing to the *Usages,* Mark signed, "That is a lot of bull manure." I had to think a moment; then it dawned on me that he meant bullshit. Mark invented other curse words with signs and all the novices seemed to know what he meant. He didn't care for Father Mary and let everyone know it frequently. He felt we were treated like young ladies in a finishing school. That thought would never have entered my head. Not in these surroundings; not a finishing school!

James, a friend of Mark, was a chaotic, restless novice, an ex-marine who had had a religious conversation while attending Catholic University in Washington, DC, which led him to the monastery. He was always enthusiastic about some cause, usually for changes, and against the present regime. He wore me out with his over-enthusiastic sign making. But I liked him; he was the first person I had ever met from Brooklyn, New York and a brutally honest and charming character.

All of this humanness among the brethren was reassuring in a way but, being self-righteous and judgmental, I was somewhat dismayed. This was not what I had expected! However, I thought prayer, work, meditation, and self-denial would surely lead to peace and union with God, and the likeness to Christ I had dreamed of. These novices were searching for God in their own way. I had warm feelings toward all of them.

I was waiting for a letter from home. Father Mary told me all my mail would be opened by the Prior (second in command) and any money or anything else objectionable or distracting would be removed from the letter, especially money! Mail would be placed under my napkin in the refectory. He said I would be allowed to write home four times a year, the next date would be on August 15, the Feast of the Assumption. These letters should be dropped unsealed into the Abbot's box. I was so young and oblivious that it did not occur to me that this smacked of cultism. He then reminded me that no visits from family or friends were allowed during the first year.

II

Lauds: Dawn of a New Day

Lauds means "praises." It is chanted at daybreak in joyous response to God's bounty, which surrounds us.

I was getting used to the regime and it was nearing time for me to take the habit, receive a new name, and become a novice monk. The ceremony of "clothing" was held in the Chapter Room. The Abbot blessed the white habit and prayed for the one who would wear it. He took off my secular jacket saying, "Take off the old man." He then put the white robe over my head, saying, "Put on the new man in Christ Jesus. May God complete in you the work He has begun, Frater Mary Gabriel," (my new name). A new name was a symbol of leaving old ways behind and assuming a new identity. Indeed, I felt like a new man!

After Chapter, I went to my cell and discarded all my secular clothes including underwear and socks. There was a bundle of new underclothes on my bed. I put on the large canvas drawers that tied at the waist and below the knees, with leggings that covered the heel, and separate foot pieces like booties. Over the underwear went the white cotton robe, a white scapular (an apron-like thing) that hung down in the front and back with a hood, and a white cloth belt. Over all that we had a white-hooded cloak that was always worn in Church and in the house, except during the hottest months.

I went to the basement where a brother was waiting to shave my head. I became queasy, seeing all my thick brown hair, which I had always nurtured, falling to the floor. I thought, *I could never leave now with a bald head.* After it was over, I felt like a real monk and I went upstairs to join the other novices. A couple of them laughed as I walked in. One of them signed, "You look different."

I signed back, "The same as you." These were my brothers for better or for worse. We all resembled each other, at least externally.

Coming in from work that afternoon, I headed for the shower, took off my work clothes and, and after a hot shower, put on the nice clean new white habit and headed upstairs toward the Chapel. Father Mary appeared and beckoned me into his office. He asked if I had been taking a shower. I told him I had. He explained that now that I was a novice monk I would only be allowed to take a shower once a week. I was devastated. No wonder there was the aroma of sweat when we gathered in the same room. I went to the Chapel, knelt down and prayed, "Lord, the food is horrible, the bed is horrible, and I accept it all for you. But, Lord, I don't think I can take *this!*"

The Holy Rule of St. Benedict says that a monk should always be ready day and night to rise and go to the service of His Master. The Trappists interpreted that to mean that you should sleep fully dressed in your habit (except for shoes) so that when the rising bell rang you could jump up and be all ready to go to the Chapel without delay to praise God in community prayer.

Now imagine this: underwear and socks washed once a week, robes once a month, and you were supposed to sleep fully dressed. Pretty unsanitary! But the Trappists of the old days considered it "not pampering the body."

I never slept fully dressed in my habit—even in the novitiate days. That was one rule I refused to keep. I got by with it until someone proclaimed me in the Chapter of Faults for sleeping without my habit on. I thought, *How does he know that?* I guessed my curtain blew open as he was passing by. Anyway, the Abbot smiled and said, "See me after Chapter, son."

When I went over to his office, the Abbot said, "Son, I know how you feel about sleeping in the habit. I don't sleep in mine either! That rule goes back to the old days of unreasonable austerity. And besides, it is unsanitary. I want you to go to the wardrobe keeper and tell him to give you a white robe split up the back. That way, when you sleep in it, it will look like you are clothed if anyone should see into your cell." So now I had monastic pajamas, a robe for sleeping.

Much later, the fire alarm went off during the night and we all evacuated the dormitory. As I was hastening down the steps with all the other monks, someone behind me taped me on the shoulder and signed, "Your back end is showing." I suddenly remembered that my robe was split up the back and my butt was in full view of everyone behind me. Strangely, I was never proclaimed in Chapter of Faults for this. Maybe they didn't know exactly how to put into words what they had seen that night. . . .

I heard that the Abbot General of the Order, Dom Gabriel Sortais, would be coming from France to visit us soon. I immediately started thinking of asking his permission for a daily shower. Sure enough, when the Abbot General came he interviewed each monk. When my turn came, I begged him to allow me to take a daily shower. My request had to be translated into French and he looked as if he did not understand. He and the translator, Father Nicolas, started a heated discussion in French and the Abbot General was flailing his arms around. I only understood the words, "Mon Dieu."

At last, Father Nicolas explained to me in English, "The Abbot General is horrified that the monks in the USA do not take a shower but once a week. He thought Americans were clean! This explained the smell he noticed at Gethsemani," (our mother monastery). Apparently this rule was a holdover from the early French monks of the 1800s who came from France. Father Nicolas said the Abbot General was ordering our Abbot to unlock the showers and to allow everyone to have a daily shower if he wished. Meanwhile, I was invited to come to the Guesthouse and use his shower anytime I wanted, twice a day if I wished, while he was there.

The Abbot General said he had suffered more from the heat in Georgia than he had in Africa! He suggested taking down the partitions in the dormitory and even installing air-conditioning. Unfortunately, these suggestions were not followed.

Recently, while reading *The Waters of Siloe* by Thomas Merton, I learned some interesting things about this Abbot General of our Order who had been so kind to me as an eighteen-year-old novice. He had been a French soldier in the Twenty-Fifth Infantry Motorized Division during World War II and was wounded in action. He was taken prisoner by the Nazis, and starved for a winter in a prison camp in Prussia. In 1941, he returned to his monastery to spend the rest of the war in the quiet routine of Cistercian life. He later became the Abbot General of the whole Order.

I was beginning to feel at home in this environment despite all. I was not critical of most rules and regulations. For example, it never occurred to me that it was somewhat hypocritical to keep silence yet talk to each other with signs. Nor was I insulted when Father Mary told me my work habit was too short (it should come below the knees), that we do not cross our legs, or that you must always ask someone (whoever was around at the time) for permission to take a drink of water. Also, you should never sit down at a table in the Scriptorium next to someone who was ahead of you in seniority until that person nodded, giving you permission to sit.

None of these things fazed me. It was all part of humility, along with keeping the eyes lowered and not looking around. Although at eighteen it was not likely that I would really practice "custody of the eyes," as it was called. I saw everything!

Every Friday morning after Lauds we went to the dormitory, pulled down the curtain of our cells, stripped to the waist, took out a whip of seven tails made of heavy nylon cords with knots in it, and beat ourselves on the back. The Prior would recite one of the longer Psalms in the Psalter (it seemed endless at times). This was really only a symbol of "subduing the body," but it did hurt.

All of this may sound as crazy to you as it does to me, too, years later. At the time, I was so intent on being holy, getting rid of selfishness and sin that I never rebelled. The ultimate purpose of monastic life was "mystical union with God." All the self-denial and all the prayer, reading, and study were supposed to be conducive to "recollection," i.e., awareness of God. I was striving diligently for this. I read books such as *The Presence of God* by Brother Lawrence, *Abandonment to Divine Providence* by de Causade, *The Imitation of Christ* by Thomas à Kempis and, of course, Holy Scripture, especially John's Gospel. Love for and devotion to the Blessed Virgin Mary was part of every monk's life and that was a great consolation for me also.

Strangely enough, novices were not allowed to read the writings of John of the Cross or Teresa of Avila (both great mystics of the Church). The reason given was that since we had not had much experience in the spiritual life we might imagine mystical experiences that were not real.

We were warned of two other dangers. The first was straining, i.e., trying too hard to remain focused and recollected. The second was against particular friendships, i.e., forming a special bond with a confrere you really liked more than others. You should have a general fraternal charity for everyone but not a particular friend. Once Frater James (from Brooklyn) signed to me with some whispering, "I'm sick of all this fraternal charity, all I want is someone to love me." Then he snarled disgustedly. I was terribly scandalized at his attitude.

I was finding it difficult to deal with some of the brothers, but always kept up a good front, smiling and being friendly to everyone. Several novices once made fun of me for smiling all the time, indicating I was a Pollyanna. I really was worried that they thought

I was a phony, but I didn't feel like a phony. I was in dead earnest—smiles and all!

During the novitiate days I felt tremendous consolation in prayer. Jesus was very real to me and I felt God's presence daily. The beauty of the chant, the dignity of the community Mass where we received Holy Communion, the flowing white cowls and cloaks of the monks created a spiritual atmosphere for prayer. I was happy.

Father Mary warned us that these feelings would pass away and someday we would have to live by faith alone. I hoped that day would be a long way off. I dreaded that bleak prospect and clung to these feelings of warmth and sweetness that came frequently. Maybe Father Mary was wrong—but deep down I knew he was right.

Father Abbot, Dom Robert McGann, was a man of great simplicity and down-to-earthness. He did not encourage spiritual athletics, but rather moderation in everything. Charity was the greatest virtue. Compassion developed in community life, faithfulness to the Divine Office, personal prayer and a good dose of hard work performed well were the ingredients of monastic life. And he used to say that he wished there were an eighth sacrament to give us common sense. He was always available for spiritual help. When you knocked on his door he would stomp his big foot, which meant "come in." He was almost always there, or somewhere nearby.

He reminded me of a Sea Captain in total command of his ship. (By the way, he had a big blurred tattoo on his right forearm that I could never get a good look at. His sleeve would slip up and I could see the blue but I couldn't figure out what the picture was. I wondered if it was a mermaid tattoo!) When he was present, I felt safe, secure, understood, and cared for. He was always ready to listen carefully and give encouragement. He called everyone son. He had been a monk at Gethsemani since he was sixteen years old, fresh from Ireland by way of New York City.

24

Father Dom Robert McGann, O.C.S.O., second Abbot of Conyers, was a real father to the monks, a man of great wisdom, and a true man of prayer.

I don't think I am exaggerating the spirituality that we were striving to live. Though it may sound artificial and contrived, it was based on a long history of monastic *ascesis,* which means an austere simple "way" to God. Let me digress here for a few minutes and tell you a little about the monastic traditions and the origins of the Trappists, the Order of Cistercians of the Strict Observance.

The History of the Trappists

Back in the fifth century, St. Benedict of Nursia wrote a rule for monks living in community. The word monk means "alone." He is one who lives alone with God in a community of solitaries. This rule outlined a very practical, simple way for men to put into practice the teachings of Jesus in everyday life. It was a school of holiness, prayer and work, charity and humility. Living in community was meant to foster the peace of Christ that surpasses all understanding. Monasteries often had written over their gates, "Pax Entrantibus," (Peace to all who enter here).

Over the centuries, the followers of St. Benedict created oases of learning and spirituality throughout Europe, preserving civilization and Christianity during the dark ages. In the process of all of this, monasteries often became centers of power and influence. They became wealthy and somewhat relaxed in the observance of the Holy Rule. At least that is how St. Robert, the Abbot of Molesmes in France, felt. He left his Benedictine monastery and went to an isolated piece of land to start a new monastery along with two fellow monks, Alberic and Stephen, and a few followers. The Pope, himself a Benedictine monk, ordered Robert back to his original monastery. Alberic took over the reigns of the new monastery. The Pope asked the Cistercians, as they are now called, to change the color of their habit and become a separate Order from the Benedictines.

This new Order, living such an austere life of prayer, penance, and separation from the world, was not attracting recruits at first. Then one day a young man named Bernard appeared with thirty of his relatives and friends seeking admission. Thus began the glorious days of the Cistercian Order.

St. Bernard was a brilliant preacher and a man of prayer, inspiring his monks to holiness of life and dedication. The monk was a man who gave himself completely to the worship of God, a visible witness to the transcendence of God. Seeking God alone, leaving all worldly desires and pursuits behind, his life was completely hidden in Christ. In an age of faith, these monks were seen as exemplars of complete self-giving to God. Their lives brought blessings to all around them and their prayers were sought after. Soon they were scattered all over Europe. Right before the Reformation, there were about 745 monasteries in France, England, Spain and Italy. These monks also had become experts in agriculture and cattle raising.

As the time went on the Cistercian Order also became influential and powerful. Before the death of St. Bernard they had already produced one Pope, Eugenius III, a monk from St. Bernard's own Abbey of Clariveaux. As the Order became wealthier, relaxation of the rules set in. There were many reasons for this but the greatest was the practice of bestowing ownership of monasteries to men who had no interest in fostering religious life but only in bringing in money for themselves from the farms and cattle of the Abbey. These people were called Abbots in Commendam. So many Abbeys became homes for small groups of disenchanted monks who did nothing much but live there.

A man named Jean Armand de Rancé had inherited one such Abbey when he was very young. There are strange tales about his sudden conversion. They center on his fiancée's death. One such tale said that he saw her laid out several days after her death and she had begun to decompose. Whatever it was, something dramatic happened that caused de Rancé to abandon his life of worldly pursuits. He had no monastic training and had grown up as a courtier with no exposure to monasticism. After living a while in an observant monastery, he went to his own monastery of La Trappe and started reforming it.

With almost fanatical zeal, he enforced a more rigorous observance than had ever been seen before. He enforced complete silence, early rising, hard work in the fields, chanting of the Divine Office eight times a day, sleeping on straw and boards, constant fasting, a life of prayer, penance, and separation from the world. The monks ate their first meal after Vespers (about 4 P.M.). It has been claimed that the average life span of a Trappist in the first days of La Trappe was about three years and that most of the monks died of lung disease or malnutrition. These monks were still Cistercians despite their incredibly radical observances and they attracted vocations gradually.

One of the Popes, Leo XIII, finally recognized that now there were two Cistercian Orders. He decreed that one be called the Sacred Order of Citeaux and the other the Cistercians of the Strict Observance. The Sacred Order of Citeaux had sometimes taken on teaching and parish work for various reasons. The Strict Observance consisted not only of La Trappe, but also other Cistercian monasteries that had reformed and were following a stricter observance. These reformed houses became one congregation, some of them having to sacrifice some of their austerities and become more moderate.

The Trappist Monastery at Conyers, Georgia (which I have been describing) was a descendant of La Trappe by way of Mt. Mellary in France, which founded Gethsemani Abbey in Bardstown, Kentucky. Gethsemani had the reputation of being one of the strictest houses in the Cistercian Order. In March 1944, Gethsemani Abbey sent twenty monks to Conyers, Georgia to start a new monastery, Our Lady of the Holy Ghost. These twenty monks moved into a spacious old cow barn which they converted into a Chapel, a dormitory, and Scriptorium. Their kitchen and refectory were in the sheds surrounding the barn.

These monks were strangers. Their neighbors in rural Georgia and the local folks did not know what to think of the hooded men in white robes who had moved into their neighborhood. There were rumors that prisoners were being held in the barn against their will. The local law officials were sent to investigate and found nothing amiss.

As the days went by, the people saw their silent neighbors laboring in the fields and building a temporary wooden monastery in a cotton field. They began to admire and respect these hard-working men and were soon glad to have them in their midst. The crude quarters of the monks and the incredible amount of work involved made their lives harder than anything they had ever experienced at Gethsemani. The tremendous heat of the Georgia summer gained for the new monastery the popular title, "Our Lady of the Frying Pan." I'm indebted to Thomas Merton's *Waters of Siloe* for some of this information.

More Novitiate

Back to my story. During my first year of novitiate, new frater postulants came aboard. One small blond-haired man, who had been a Marine and later an architectural major at Catholic University of America, entered after me. He took the name Otis. The new novice took a great interest in the three big volumes of Garrigou-La Grange on the spiritual life and I knew immediately he was an intellectual. He was also quite gifted musically and artistically. He would become a major advisor in the building of the new Abbey Church and he was the artist who designed stained-glass windows for the church and then established a stained-glass department making windows for churches all over the USA. Of course, that was after he had made his final vows. He seemed very self-assured, always competent, always in control. I felt very inferior to him. He always seemed to know so much about everything. He was never wrong about anything. I liked him despite that!

The days became routine and I now felt that I was a member of a family. We all dressed alike, ate together, worked together, and prayed together. I was looking forward to becoming a fully professed monk (when you take the vows of poverty, chastity, obedience, and conversion of manners and stability). These vows are supposed to free you of worldly cares so that you belong entirely to God. Chastity meant detachment and purity of heart; poverty, freedom from wealth and things; obedience, freedom from power and prestige, stability; belonging to one community for life.

Conversion of manners meant constant striving for holiness. (I never quite understood what this last vow really meant, but I knew it was something good.) Some monks interpreted it as a vow to always do the more perfect thing. I did not believe that. That would be impossible. I took it to mean that conversion is an ongoing process. A monk vowed to live out his conversion day by day.

We were instructed three times a week on the spirituality of the vows, Scripture, and the traditions and the Usages of the Order. Every evening before night prayers, Father Mary gave points for the next morning's meditation time. These were his own thoughts on the parables of Jesus and on His life. We took notes. It was often hard to pay attention to his monotone voice and it was hard to keep awake the next morning to meditate. It was also difficult to take notes because we were not allowed to own a pen. We had to use one from a common box on the table (the old dip-in-the-ink kind) and our paper consisted of old envelopes sewn together. All of this in the name of poverty. For the same reason, we were not allowed to have a wristwatch and even the books we were allowed to have were always called "our" books. For handkerchiefs, we had large pieces of cloth from feed sacks of bright red checks that contrasted greatly with the white habit when a monk took one out to blow his nose.

Once again, legalistic observances did not bother me at all. I must confess that several times I tried to speak verbally to another novice and each time I was rebuffed with a look of horror. One time Brother Leo drove a tractor straight at me and thought it was funny. I deliberately broke silence and yelled at him some angry words (and was proclaimed for it) and I'm sure such impetuousness scandalized the brethren.

Dom Robert said one day in Chapter, "We have guests in the dormitory, everyone take your mattress outside in the sun today and clean and spray the cells with insecticide." *Oh, no—on top of everything we had bugs in our beds!* No one seemed to make much of it. In fact, my Confessor told me that this was nothing compared to the old days at Gethsemani when monks sometimes had lice. He said Father Henry, a blind monk, was his Confessor and he often saw lice crawling up out of Father Henry's habit, but never once saw him scratch or swat at them. That was part of the heroic sanctity for which he was known, I guess.

Novices were given an indulgence, some extra food during the winter fast (from September 14 until Easter). One evening I noticed little creatures, floating legs up, in my Cream of Wheat. I glanced at Frater Denis' bowl and he was quickly gobbling up Cream of Wheat, bugs and all, without revulsion. Such heights of sanctity were beyond me! Besides, I didn't remember the New Testament or the Holy Rule commending those who ate bugs without retching.

The Dormitory

Brother Ambrose entered the Trappists at the age of sixty-eight. He had owned a cigar shop in a small town in Iowa and raised eleven children. One of his sons was a priest in our community, two of his sons were Benedictines at Atchison, Kansas, and one daughter was a Carmelite nun at Carmel, California. His youngest son had entered our community, but did not stay long. The rest of his children got married and produced families. Despite all that, Brother Ambrose seemed to be a jolly fellow. The first night he was there (a Georgia summer night) all the monks were turning and tossing in their hot miserable cells trying to get to sleep. Brother Ambrose suddenly called out in his sleep at the top of his voice, "Come on, Joe. Let's go down to the corner and get an ice-cold beer." Monks laughed all over the dorm. They probably thought it was a good idea! This sleeping in an open dormitory was fraught with inconveniences.

Father Peter was a real problem for me in the dorm. He had a lot of trouble with catarrh and sometimes he would cough at night. One night I kept dozing off and each time I would get to sleep, he would start up again with loud coughing. This must have happened once, when I had fallen into a deep sleep, and I threw my huge rosary beads against the wall and yelled, "Shut up, you son of a bitch!" This was followed by complete silence until the bell rang at 2 A.M. When I stepped out of my cell, Frater Bernard who slept next to me made the sign, "Congratulations," and cracked up laughing. That monk later became an Abbot.

The Abbot called me over the next day and said, "Son, did you call Father Peter a son of a bitch last night in the dormitory?"

"Yes," I said.

"Why would you do that?"

I wriggled around, apologized to the Abbot and told him I was half asleep, but I would apologize to Father Peter. He laughed gently.

The Abbot told me that he had heard from my neighbors in the dormitory that I sang songs in my sleep. He said that "Dark Town Strutter's Ball" was one of most repeated songs. He then asked, "Who is this Miss Conner you talk to in your sleep?"

"She was the mother of one of my girlfriends," I replied.

"That's alright, son, I'm just kidding you. Go in peace and go easy on Father Peter."

One of the monks wrote me this note about my nightly singing in the dormitory on the occasion of my profession of simple vows:

August 20
Feast of St. Bernard

Dear Frater Gabriel,

Congratulations on winning the fight with the world, the flesh, the devil, and Billy Nolan.

I'll expect your nocturnal serenades—impromptu in character as they may be and notwithstanding same—to take on a more liturgical character, young man! I'll be listening!

The compliments with which I might ply you on such an occasion will pass with everything else except that the esteem I have for you will always remind me to keep you in my prayers and perhaps Our Lord will remember them.

May He more than suffice for you, my dear brother in Christ, for the rest of your days.

Father M. Bernadine

That is real fraternal charity, considering that I was probably waking him up with those serenades!

Brother Richard was in charge of the mattresses for the dormitory. When they got too soft or saggy he would refill them with straw, and tamp it in good and hard. I hated that straw mattress. It had taken me about a year to make an impression on it and to get my pillow loosened up. One afternoon, I came in from work and discovered that my mattress had been re-stuffed by Brother Richard; it was hard as a rock.

The next morning at Matins I was itchy all over. It became unbearable and I went to the infirmary. The infirmarian said I had a rash all over my body from top to bottom. He had never seen anything like this and that I should go to the doctor in Conyers.

33

Someone drove me in. The doctor looked at the rash and said, "Frater, you have chicken mites in every pore of your body." All my clothes had to be burned. I had to soak three times a day for several days in a chemical to kill the mites. I thought of using some obscene words on Brother Richard. Fraternal charity prevailed—at least externally. I don't think he ever knew it happened.

Liturgy

Christmastime was coming. The Advent Liturgy was beautiful. The prayers stirred deep desire for a new coming of Christ in our hearts and in our world. As a new novice, this period of anticipation was a symbol for me of looking forward to what God would accomplish in my life in the days to come.

Father Mary had told me it was against the rule in the novitiate to waste time by painting, drawing, or carving wood (which I loved to do). Later he gave me the great joy of helping Father Stephen, a young priest who was an artist, work on Christmas decorations for the Chapel. Stephen was now engaged in building a gigantic stained glass window out of paper. Everything that Stephen did, with his expansive personality, was gigantic. He created a thirty-foot-tall concrete statue of St. Benedict for one side of the new monastery. Stephen was a happy-go-lucky person with a great sense of humor and a loud laugh. I loved working with him. He later fell to his death in a tragic accident while on leave of absence from the monastery. He fell over a thousand feet into the Grand Canyon.

On Christmas Eve, Stephen and I were working together when I got a note telling me to go the Abbot's office. The Abbot said my mother and father were down at the ladies' Guesthouse. He would allow me to go down to visit with them for a few hours. Then he gently, almost apologetically, reminded me that novices were not allowed visitors for the first year but he was letting me go since they were already here.

When my mother saw me she was visibly upset. After we had hugged and kissed, she said that I looked so thin and that the shaved head and bulky habit looked terrible. My father looked more disgusted than sad. He once said to one of my sisters, "What a waste of a man's life." And I knew he really felt that way. But my concern was for my mother. This was so hard for her. She had brought me some presents: books and candy. I did not tell her that I couldn't keep them but rather acted really happy to receive them. The three hours were up and as my father and mother drove away down the road, I stood there and watched, tears running down my face. I knew that my father would be saying terrible things to my mother and this made the parting even more painful. I felt so sorry for her.

Back at the monastery I entered through the back of the Chapel where there was a smaller Chapel for visitors. Through a grill you could see the monks gathering for Vespers of Christmas Eve. I knelt down before a Nativity set that had been set up back there, put my head down, and began to cry my eyes out. I felt a soft hand on my shoulder and an elderly French Diocesan priest who was visiting the monastery said, "He has suffered for you." I was grateful for his kindness. I stood up and went to the door where there was a sign that said, "Cloister: Do not enter." I paused a moment considering the sign, thinking how hard this life was and that maybe I had made a mistake, and then stepped inside for first Vespers of Christmas Day.

At about 11:30 P.M. we were awakened by Christmas hymns being played over the loud speaker throughout the house, rather than by the usual bell. Midnight Mass was a glorious celebration. I felt so close to God and close to these people I lived and prayed with, but I was still feeling the pain of loss of my loved ones.

In my young mind I thought, *This is the price I must pay.* Later when I read Bonhoeffer's words that grace is free but not cheap, I knew exactly what he meant. The grace of this vocation was costly. Maybe the cost of discipleship was too much for me.

Fraters James and Mark, who disliked Father Mary so vehemently, must have really been in the Christmas spirit. They decided to decorate the Novice Scriptorium for Christmas and have a little party as a surprise for Father Mary. Somehow they got hold of some cookies and candy. I can't imagine where or how they got them. Father Mary was in his office, and heard lots of laughing and banging around in the Novitiate.

The party was ready as he walked in the room. Red and green streamers, a couple of poinsettias and twenty novices stood around, smiling and greeted him singing, "We wish you a Merry Christmas." Father Mary looked at everyone, surprised and then irritated. Actually, he was furious. He demanded that we take the food to the kitchen and remove the crepe paper. This was totally out of the spirit of monasticism and it fell into the category of dissipation! So ended the party and everyone departed in silence. The rest of the day was especially signless. Fraters Mark and James apologized to Father Mary a few days later. The next year on Christmas Eve, Father Mary posted a sign in the Novitiate saying, "Please do not repeat the behavior that you engaged in last year on Christmas Eve."

In the monastery Christmas didn't end on the twenty-fifth of December—but rather a season began, celebrating the Incarnation of God's Son. There was an Octave and a series of feast days called "Feasts of Sermon" (because one of the priest monks would preach a Sermon at morning Chapter). On some Feasts of Sermon, we got up at 1:30 A.M. and, on especially big feasts, we rose at 1 A.M. because all of the prayers were sung and it took much longer. Also, we had raisin bread, real butter, and secular coffee on those days. Christmas decorations disappeared slowly and you didn't notice it.

After Epiphany, the weeks faded into the Feast of the Purification, February 2, which was the end of the season. Sometime in

February or March, Lent would begin. We really lived the cycle of the liturgy. We prayed the mysteries of Christ's life in choir, meditated on them, and tried to live them. Everything was so real, so much part of everyday life.

I am describing the reactions of an immature monk who had definite illusions about monastic life: a nebulous, mystical concept of holiness and of a life somewhat unearthly. Already in the Novitiate, I was finding a life that was down to earth, simple, honest, hard but good, lived by men who were strong-minded individuals with all the ragged edges that we all share. For the first time, I was beginning to see myself and life itself more honestly. There was no escape from reality here. The kind of monastic life I had imagined did not exist. This was much better. This was what Christ meant when he said, "Take up your cross and follow me." I was trying hard.

My biggest trial and greatest joy was community life. We had absolutely no privacy. Some monks were difficult to live with and my thoughts were harsh toward them. However, community life was teaching me how to live in a charity that went way beyond politeness and civility. St. Benedict described it by saying, "This then is the good zeal which monks must foster with fervent love. They should each try to be the first to show respect to the other, supporting with the greatest patience one another's weaknesses of body or behavior, and earnestly competing in obedience to one another. No one is to pursue what he judges better for himself but, instead, what he judges better for someone else. To their fellow monks they show the pure love of brothers; to God, loving fear, to the Abbot, the unfeigned and humble love of sons. Let them prefer nothing whatever to Christ, and may He bring us all together to everlasting life." What a beautiful ideal!

One of the Abbot's homey sayings was, "We are rough stones being polished smooth by daily rubbing against each other." Some of those stones sure rubbed me the wrong way and I'm sure I rubbed some of them the wrong way, but the saying didn't make it any easier.

Along with that, daily rising at 2 A.M. retiring at 7 P.M., working on the farm, and chanting the Psalms day in and day out was not romantic.

When Lent rolled around a purple curtain was put in front of the main altar and only opened for Mass (don't ask me why!). The meals were more meager every day. We were not allowed cheese or milk, we only received a bowl of soup on Fridays, and bread and water on Good Friday. On Ash Wednesday, the ashes were placed on top of our shaven heads in the shape of a huge cross. That morning after Chapter, each monk was given a book to read during Lent at a special time each afternoon. It was always an inspirational book of some kind, sometimes quite dull—the kind you would never choose to read on your own.

Holy Week was an ordeal. All the ceremonies were different and there was often confusion among the monks. On Good Friday we went barefoot all day. After Matins we went to our cells and flogged ourselves. We chanted the whole Psalter from Psalm 1 to Psalm 150 without a break in Chapter that morning. It took almost three hours. I ate a lot of bread, thinking it would keep me from getting to hungry, but it only bloated my stomach causing it to growl and make me miserable. In the afternoon we had another service commemorating the Death of Jesus on the Cross (the Mass of the Pre-Sanctified). At the end of the day I sat barefoot, dazed, feeling like *I* had been crucified.

Lent ended at noon on Holy Saturday. The bells rang and lilies appeared all over the place. The celebration of Easter began. We had cheese and milk for supper for the first time in forty days. The liturgical season was always reflected in our meals.

A Seasoned Novice

One year of novitiate was over. During the second year, novices were allowed to study Latin grammar in preparation for Philosophy and Theology when all the texts would be written in Latin. In high school I had taken four years of Latin but did not feel fluent in the language. Those classes made it possible for us to talk to the professor but not to each other. The teacher was our first personal contact with any of the professed monks other than Father Mary.

Father Eutropius, the long, lean, bony-cheeked man who taught Latin was young but walked in a cramped and stiff-looking way. When not teaching, he spent most of his time in a room in the infirmary. He was there because he had a bad back. It seems he claimed to be in poor health all the time and was not highly regarded in the community. He and I became great friends. He took the novices out to work most days. He could be lively and funny but I sensed a deep unhappiness in him. He seemed to be a sad and broken man, but he never spoke of anything like that, only about his physical pains. He was a great help to me when I was down in the dumps. I think it was his pain that attracted me to him. I wanted to console him and we enjoyed each other's company despite a gentle reprimand to me by Father Mary.

"Ora et Labora" (Pray and Work) was the motto of Benedictine life. I was doing okay with praying, but work was another story. Mr. Ray was the "secular" in charge of the building of the new monastery. He was a licensed contractor. He was devoted to the monks but our ignorance and incompetence in the face of construction tried his patience! He often saved our lives. The Prior sent Denis, Bruno, George and me to take down the forms from the inside of a reservoir we were building. As we were just about to take away the last five or ten two-by-four supports, Mr. Ray appeared looking down in the tank frantically yelling for us to get out. We scrambled up the ladder and got out. He told us that the forms would have fallen and killed us all if we had removed three more supports.

Another time at work the Prior told the monks to each grab a leg of a high scaffold and on command to walk forward with it (this would prevent having to take it apart and reassemble it ten feet down the line). We all obeyed with misgivings and as we started to move, the whole scaffolding began to sway and was about to collapse on top of us when Mr. Ray appeared yelling at us, "Stop! Stand still!" Then he managed to get us safely out of danger.

I was sure that Mr. Ray groaned whenever he saw me coming on the job to help. He knew that I couldn't really do anything constructive and he had to figure out something to keep me out of the way, which usually meant pulling nails out of used wood. I was pretty good at that.

Farm work was simpler. Father Lawrence directed me to plow a field with a mule, assuming I would know how. Another monk helped me to get the mule ready and attach the plow. I walked behind the mule with the plow off the ground not knowing what I should do. As the mule and I reached the edge of the field, I thought it would be logical to stick the blade of the plow in the ground. The mule didn't like it and started jerking and zigzagging all over, pulling the plow and me with him. I was completely out of control. Father Lawrence came running after us yelling for me to stop, but I don't know how. He finally caught up with us and grabbed the reins, pushed me out of the way, stopped the mule, and glared at me. Then he said, "Come over here and hoe weeds," and handed me the hoe. I took the hoe and charged toward the first patch of weeds I saw, determined to redeem myself. I went after them furiously, dirt flying in all directions. Father Lawrence came running over, very agitated. I thought, *What now?*

He yelled, "Stop! Those are not weeds; those are my turnips!" I was a complete failure at farming. Father Lawrence took the hoe and showed me how to use it, i.e., inserting hoe in ground and pulling it toward you. Then he said, "You are obviously a city boy. Maybe we can find something else for you to do."

We had 11,000 chickens in a couple of chicken houses. We sold the eggs to some company. The brother in charge had arranged the nests of the hens so that when they laid eggs, they would roll out of the nests onto a conveyor belt. When the belt was turned on, you stood at the end of the belt and they all came toward you, you then took them off the belt inserting them in dividers and stacking them in boxes. I was directed to stand before the belt; the brother in charge turned it on and left.

These thousands of eggs came straight toward me. I was stacking as fast I could but eggs were dropping all around me. The more they dropped, the more I panicked. I was slipping in egg whites and yolks, thinking, *This is not contemplative work,* when all of a sudden the brother in charge came running up, sliding in egg slime; he reached down toward the ground and turned off the switch. All the eggs stopped. The brother looked at me in silence. After a few seconds he made a sign, "Go home!" I had failed again and had wasted all those eggs. I'm sure that cost the monastery some revenue.

One day when we were picking corn away from the monastery at the end of the work period, all the monks piled on a truck, pulled up their hoods, and rode away. Only Brother Leo and I were left. He showed me two huge tractors and signed, "You and I will drive them home." I gasped and signed to him that I couldn't drive. He signed, "Peace," then showed me how to get up on the seat, turned on the engine, pointed to the gas pedal signing, "Go," and to the brake signing, "Stop," and to the other gadgets signing, "Don't touch." Off we went.

My tractor was jerking and shaking, staying in low gear. The traffic on Highway 212 was sparse and the few cars that saw us coming pulled off to the side of the road and watched us go by. Some of the other novices saw me coming into the monastery grounds on a creeping tractor jerking and shaking. The Novice

Master bawled me out for this performance. I was never again allowed to touch farm equipment. I was really embarrassed.

I did a fine job shoveling cow manure, and the brothers at the cow barn were glad to have me since they had to clean up after 300 cows. Also, rubbing concrete on the new building turned out to be a great job for me. Hot in the summer and freezing in the winter. The hardest part was stripping forms off; the rest required no thinking, just rubbing with a Carborundum stone. Labor filled a good part of the day and often I just endured it, waiting for it to be over!

The monks that worked in the piggery on a daily basis always smelled like their charges, no matter how many times they took a shower. Standing behind one of them in the refectory was a real means of mortification and could destroy your appetite forever.

It was rumored that old Brother Clement, who was in charge of the pigs, had not had a shower in twenty years. I do not know if that was true or just a saying. Regardless, you did not want to get downwind of him on the stairs!

When he was sick in the infirmary. I thought this was a good chance to talk with the austere old gentleman. I got permission. At the time, the Order was going through some minor changes like allowing one hour more sleep, a bit more food, changes in clothing, and things called "mitigations." Out of curiosity, I asked Brother Clement if he thought we were getting soft and that possibly the Order was headed toward relaxation.

He replied in a low, mellow drawl, "I grew up on a farm. I remember leaning on my shovel, watching the first automobile in our county coming down the road and I watched it until it was clear out of sight. Now, I've lived to see jet planes and Sputnik. When I entered Gethsemani, my life was pretty much the same as it was on the farm. I was used to a vegetable diet and a straw mattress. But these young people coming to the monastery today have been used to air-conditioning, central heat, good meals, and comforts that I know nothing about. No, I don't think we are getting soft. These young men are seeking a life of prayer and sacrifice and I'm sure God is pleased with them. I thought *what a wise and gentle man.*

The urge to leave and give it all up came frequently. The austere life, the sameness of everyday, and the longing for someone to love and be close to often weighed on me. A nice warm fireplace in the winter time, an air-conditioned private room in summer, decent meals, an automobile, freedom to travel, friends and fun were visions that flashed through my head along with the usual *delectatio morosa* (the Latin phrase for dwelling on sexual fantasies). The innumerable senseless rules and petty accusations at Chapter of Faults all began to seem more and more like what Mark called "bullshit." But the hope of becoming holy, living in God's presence kept me trudging along. This idealistic, vision of my innocent young heart kept me there.

During the reign of the first Abbot of Conyers, Dom James Fox, the monks had started to build a permanent monastery under the direction of Mr. Les Ray, the contractor (that was before I arrived). The work was suspended when Dom James became the new Abbot of Gethsemani and left. When my abbot, Dom Robert McGann, had come to Conyers, he was an energetic and intelligent man of about sixty-five. He suspended work on the building for awhile for financial reasons. At the time when the work on the building resumed, I was a second-year novice. The first thing the monks had to do was jack hammer down all the brick work that had been laid on one wing because they found it would be cheaper and more practical to build out of steel reinforced concrete. This building project seemed so impossible that I thought it would never be finished, but that we would work on it every day until we all died. The novices were less involved than the others, but we helped with every big sweaty concrete pour. We mixed the sand and gravel, made the concrete on the spot, and ran up ramps with wheelbarrows (wearing cumbersome blue denim robes).

During the second year novices began to leave. Matthew, my

guardian angel, left. He had been having headaches (was straining), and was on the verge of a nervous breakdown. Mark, with the bushy eyebrows, tired of the b.s., walked out one day. James was always threatening to leave, but never did. Adam was a wild-eyed novice from Savannah, Georgia, constantly fingering his rosary, moving his lips and smiling with his eyes turned to heaven through thick glasses. One day he jumped up on the table and started preaching to the other novices, who watched in disbelief, as Father Mary got him down from the table and hauled him off to the infirmary. That was the last we saw of Adam; however, we heard he often preached on the street corners of Savannah after he left us.

The choir novices did not see the lay brother novices very often because they had a separate schedule and separate quarters. Their Novice Master was a dear elderly priest from Bavaria, Father Ephrem. He ran a tight ship. A terribly sad thing happened in the brother's novitiate. A tall, thin, eighteen-year-old brother novice named Octavius had been acting strangely and claimed he was the reincarnation of Elijah. A psychiatrist in Atlanta was treating him, but at some point there was so much concern about his health that he was confined to the infirmary, waiting to be sent to Council Bluffs, Iowa for treatment. All sharp objects were removed from his room and monks took turns sitting outside his door all night so that he would not run away. When the priests started to say the morning Masses at 4 A.M. there was a change of shifts and somehow Octavius got out of his room and disappeared. The Abbot asked all the monks to scour the farm. Finally, one brother remembered that Brother Octavius used to go up inside the silo to read and pray. The brother in charge of the cow barn went up the ladder on the silo, which was covered by a metal hood; there was only room for one person under it. When he looked over into the silo, he saw Brother Octavius' body swinging from a rope. He quickly got down, called the Prior to come see the ghastly sight, and to call the coroner from Conyers.

The day of the tragedy, a professed monk stood before me in

the refectory and signed, "Go watch with dead." I was surprised, but acted casual as if this were routine, asked permission to leave, went to the infirmary where the body was laid out and sat down to pray the Psalms. This was the first time I had ever seen a dead body that had not been made up to look alive the way they do in the funeral home. Brother O's face was a dusky color. His lips were greenish white. It was an eerie sight. He was not embalmed and had no cosmetic treatment. He was plain dead. I remembered how he had looked on that awful night when he was going to hang himself because, as I was going upstairs, I met him briefly. He signed "God alone," and kept going. This was before anyone knew that he had run away; I had no idea what he was doing. These thoughts were going through my mind as I sat praying beside his body.

The other monk who had been praying got up and left. I glanced up at the corpse, prayed and glanced up over and over. On one glance up I caught sight of a priest monk glaring at me from the door leading into the patient rooms. I recognized him as a priest who had been in and out of mental institutions and had been violent on occasion. Leering at me, he signed, "Do you want to go to Heaven with brother?"

I swallowed hard and signed back, "Not now. Not now." I was fervently praying that he would leave.

Brother Octavius's body was buried the very next day. This was the first death of a monk at Conyers. The Prior preached a beautiful homily that somehow made spiritual sense of this horrible tragedy. We would much rather have wanted our first funeral to be a joyful farewell to a monk who had lived the life for many years.

In those days monks were buried simply in their habits without even a sheet around them. Brother Octavius's parents called from out West, wanting to come to the funeral but it was already taking place. (They would later come and visit the grave, looking in from outside the enclosure.) I was badly shaken by this whole scene. The body was lowered into the grave while a brother went down into the grave and pinned shut the hood of the dead brother. Octavius's fellow novices shoveled dirt into the grave, starting at the feet, working upward. When we got back to the house and were changing clothes for work, I saw a very young brother novice, Dominic, sitting and crying hysterically. I went over, sat next to him, put my arms around him, and broke silence by speaking to him. With tears streaming down his face he said, "I can't take it. I'm cracking up!" I told him to go to the Abbot right that minute and tell him exactly that. Dominic left the very next day and later became a Salesian seminarian and eventually a priest in that community serving young people.

Shortly after that I asked permission for something to help with my nerves. The infirmarian put me on daily doses of Phenobarbital. I didn't know what it was, but I sailed through the rest of the year like a model novice!

On a bright spring morning I was just outside the enclosure fence working in a little garden pulling weeds when a black car pulled up and three women got out. I glanced out of the side of my eyes and saw women for the first time since I had entered the monastery in July—many months earlier. Their faces startled me a little. The lipstick was so red, the eyebrows so vividly drawn. Their faces looked like painted masks. I'm sure they were just ordinary women—but not having seen ordinary women for some months, I was shocked. They saw me in my monastic robe kneeling in the dirt and they immediately came over and started asking me questions. I put my finger over my lips signaling, "Silence." I had no permission to speak to them.

They looked at each other and I heard one say, "They don't speak." I smiled and one of them said "Isn't he sweet?" The chasm between the monastery and the "world" became more real than ever that day. I did not feel at all sweet, but rather irritated.

III

Prime, Terce, Sext, None: The Work Day

These are the little hours of prayer that are interspersed throughout the monks' work day.

My days as a novice were now over and I was preparing to make temporary vows for three years. But as far as I was concerned, this was for life! I would be a monk forever. The day before my profession of vows I was working in the garden in a field close to the monastery. I saw a car from Tennessee coming up the road. It was my family! I ran to the house, washed up and put on my white habit, ready to go meet my mother, father, two sisters, and one brother. On the way I met Father Mary who asked me where I was going during work period. I told him my family was here. He said, "Frater Gabriel, are you making your vows to God or to your family?"

I said, "To God," of course. Then he told me to put on my work clothes and go back to my chore in the garden. I could see my family tomorrow.

The family could not attend the ceremony because it took place in the Chapter Room in the enclosure. However, I did have time to go out to see them before the service. My white scapular was filthy, so I asked Frater Kevin, a rather effeminate novice, to lend me his nice, clean, pressed-looking scapular that he kept freshly washed all the time and neatly folded under his mattress at

Frater Gabriel and his brother Joe at the time of his simple profession.

night—thus, the pressed look. The rest of us never wore a pressed habit.

After greeting, hugging, and kissing everyone, my brother whispered, "Bill, what kind of cologne are you wearing? You smell like a French whore!" Kevin's scapular was not only clean but it bore the aroma of Chanel. I wondered where he got it since the Abbot would not let me keep deodorant when my mother packed it in a parcel of books and cookies. Dom Robert had said to me, "Son, that's effeminate!"

It was the feast of St. Bernard of Clairvaux, the great Abbot who was the glory of our Order. This day I would receive the black scapular and leather belt of the professed monk and the monastic cowl (an impractical, but beautiful, flowing white garment whose wide sleeves reached to the ground and had to be gathered up to get your hands out). This impractical garment was a symbol of contemplative life worn during all community prayers. Also, I received the monastic tonsure (the ring of hair left around the head while all the rest was shaved off). After all the blessings and the vows, I went outside the enclosure to celebrate with my family. I was now a full-fledged monk. My mother, sisters, and family members seemed so proud of me and stayed another day before leaving for Tennessee. We had a good visit and their departure was not as painful this time.

Newly professed monks stay in the Novitiate for a few weeks before moving over to the professed Scriptorium. For some reason, they kept me back for several months, probably because of my immaturity. They never said why.

The life did not change on the professed side. It was all the same except for the work assignments. Summer and winter, Fraters Denis and Bruno (the two "saints") and I were assigned the job of stripping forms from the concrete and rubbing the walls of the new building with carborundum stones, smoothing them out to a beautiful white finish. Actually, it was nice to know where you were going to work each day. We formed a team and took pride in our work.

I was also assigned the job of bell ringer, which meant waking the monks at 2 A.M. each day (I was given the luxury of a pocket watch) and ringing all the bells for all the various Offices. I was very prompt and faithful to the job. At times the large Chapel bell was known to fall from its moorings and land with a thud on the ceiling right above the bell ringer's head. I could imagine the thing coming straight through the drywall someday and demolishing me.

One morning I accidentally started ringing the rising dormitory bell at 1 A.M. instead of 2 A.M. Father Mary came running out looking horrified, signaling me to stop. The two of us stood there signing to the sleepy monks, "Go back to bed, not time yet." For penance, that day at the noon meal I knelt before the Abbot's table in the refectory with outstretched arms and begged the community for forgiveness for being so stupid as to awaken them an hour early that morning. Then I took my bowl and knelt before each monk, begging for food, and sat on the floor to eat it. Some of my classmates were laughing and making faces the whole time, but I did not think it was funny.

One of the monks, Father M. Bernard, who could not get back to sleep that morning after the premature bell, went to the Scriptorium and wrote a poem for me between 1 A.M. and 2 A.M., December 3, 1953. It was entitled, "The One O'Clock Jump." (If you wish, you can read it on page 106 of this book.)

The Work of Education

Studies for the priesthood now began in earnest. The training for the priesthood took about seven years of formal studies: three years of Philosophy, Greek, and Hebrew; and four years of Theology, Scripture, Church History, and Canon Law.

Joseph Gredt, who authored the textbooks we used for Philosophy, was a staunch disciple of Thomas Aquinas (a medieval philosopher/theologian whom the Catholic Church had sort of canonized as the Teacher of Truth, par excellence). These two huge textbooks were written by a German author in the Latin language. The sentences were long and convoluted, sometimes going on for a paragraph or so before a verb emerged to give the whole thing sense.

Fortunately, I had now had six years of Latin grammar and could figure out what the words were saying but I didn't have a clue as to what they meant. Epistemology was the first on the list, and then came Logic, Theodicy, Cosmology, Metaphysics, Ethics, and Anthropology. We also had courses in the History of Philosophy (fortunately in English), and classes in Greek and Hebrew so that we would be slightly familiar with the languages of Scripture.

Frater Otis took to Philosophy like a duck to water the very first day. He signed to me that it was not difficult and that I should be patient; it would all fall together and the light would go on. Sitting in class in a total fog made me feel anxious. Otis and others would speak up and use all the jargon and Latin phrases as if they had been born and reared using them. I used to think I was bright, but not anymore. How could I get through this?

Father Herman, the professor, was a small young man perhaps twenty-eight or so, with a ruddy complexion and a very pleasant bright smile, beginning to bald, and obviously a master of the subject he taught. For two years we had contact with Father Herman two or three times a week. I admired his clear thinking and with his help, indeed, the light did finally go on. Metaphysics, which deals with the "nature of being" or the "mystery of being" insofar as we can study it, gave me a whole new way of thinking about reality and about Ultimate Reality. My eyes were opened to a world I had never even dreamt about. In Philosophy, we were exposed to all the great thinkers down through the ages. These thinkers were critiqued in the light of Thomas Aquinas and Aristotle and always found wanting, if not downright erroneous.

At that time, the Trappists did not send monks outside to go to school to the great universities. It was rumored that the Order was anti-intellectual. I don't think that was true, but Conyers did not train monks to teach or to get Ph.D's. Our professors were usually men who had received their education elsewhere, generally in other religious orders. Father Herman had been a Holy Ghost Father, Father Paul a Paulist, Father Nicholas a Diocesan priest and Father Thomas a Dominican. We had an excellent faculty.

However, for us, studies were always secondary. First came the spiritual life and everything else was supposed to enhance that and bring you closer to God. Hauling and shoveling manure, cleaning debris from Honey Creek, concrete pours and such were essential for a monk, but intellectual pride or arrogance was not to be tolerated. For me, philosophy became a passion, and I felt it put me on more solid ground in my spiritual life. Looking back, I see that I was living "in my head" more than in the real world. I loved it. The real would could wait!

The Abbot was suspicious of the theologian Ives Congar. I was aware that he was a French Dominican who was writing some stimulating material. The Abbot was concerned about his "orthodoxy." He asked me to check our library and let him know how many of Congar's works were there. He also told me to be wary of new ideas on Scripture. He said Cornelius a Lapide was the only solid commentator I should read. But I was not eager to read the dust-covered volumes of an antiquated author.

Another Dimension of Education

As I was gaining new insights I also gained a new friend, a monk whose name was Father Charles (Jack English) who had been editor of *The Catholic Worker* for some years. He was the librarian and saw to it that I read many books that were somewhat upsetting to me, including subjects on social justice, the Church's lack of initiative in racial issues, and lack of advocacy for the poor. He pointed me to new theologians who were non-Thomistic. He seemed to be destroying my idols but I knew I needed broader vision. At times I thought perhaps he was a Communist (it was the fifties), but I knew better.

This is how I first got to talk to Charles verbally. My mother was visiting me one summer in July when Dorothy Day came to visit Father Charles. She and my mother stayed together at the ladies' Guesthouse and they got along beautifully. Of course, my mother had no idea who she was. In my guilt over lack of social concerns, I did not have much to say to her. She seemed very quiet and plain. When she left, Father Charles told me I had met a saint and then handed me more radical books from the library.

Every time Father Charles had an outstanding visitor he invited me to come to meet them. For instance, he invited me to meet Caroline Gordon, a famous author. He had already introduced me to the writings of "The Fugitives," a group of southern poets with whom she was connected. I found all of this very exciting and stimulating, but felt self-conscious and unenlightened at these visits with famous people.

In class we could talk with our theology professor, Father Herman. This often led to heated discussions and arguments, providing a platform for zeal and oratory, and flexing of intellectual muscles, just like in seminaries anywhere! There was competition and rivalry here on a minor scale.

We learned all the defined teachings of the Catholic Church from Tanqueray (the official text). We learned that many great religious leaders such as John Hus and Martin Luther were heretics. But most of all we learned that Aquinas had the right answers and the Church had the infallible answers.

Father Herman had a mellow, beautiful tenor singing voice; he was a cantor. He was handsome, talented, always appeared happy, yet there were some strange things about him. When not smiling, he looked strained because his face would turn red and drawn. He also said some peculiar things at times. He had a great devotion to St. Ann (according to popular pious tradition, she was the mother of the Virgin Mary). He made some unexpected remarks that made no sense such as how, "Mothers always gobble up the glory." Besides, the preoccupation with St. Ann seemed out of character for this brilliant man.

Then, one day Herman disappeared. He could not be contacted by the Abbot. No one ever heard from him again. He had been corresponding with a woman in another state who had once visited him and everyone assumed he had disappeared with her, but no one ever knew what became of him. Even his family could not find him.

Father Paul, our Church History Professor, was an aristocratic man from a well-to-do family. He had grown up without much religious training, living the good life. He was a sculptor and went to Yale on an art scholarship. While in Europe during research for his dissertation, the senselessness of it all overwhelmed him and he turned to God, became a devout Catholic, talked to the Paulist Fathers, and joined their community, later becoming a Trappist monk. Father Paul was a *Censor Librorum* for the Cistercian Order in the United States. That meant he had to read every book written by any American Trappist and give it his okay. You can imagine who kept him the busiest: Father Louis (Thomas Merton). He used to laugh and sometimes groan about the prolific output of this "famous author," as Merton once called himself. I asked Father Paul if he thought Merton was a saint. Paul said, "I think we need a new definition of what a saint is. Rome only canonizes those people whose lives have been examined for heroic virtue. In reality living a flawed and conflicted life can be heroic virtue. Yes, Father Louis was a saint in that sense."

Paul's Church History classes were spellbinding. I looked forward to every one of them. He knew all the small intimate details that make the lives of historical people interesting. Rather than dates and facts, we were introduced to live people. We learned of all the scandals and heresies and dirty laundry, as well as the glories of the Catholic Church for 2000 years! He wanted us to know about the scandals of Church History so that when opponents of Catholicism brought them up we would be well-informed and know their context.

I chose Father Paul as my Confessor and Spiritual Director (that's how I know all about him) and my weekly meetings not only helped me grow spiritually, but they introduced me to the finer things of life such as good taste in art and music. In a word, he shared his cultural background with me. His homilies in Chapter were short, concise, and always excellent. I thought that's the way one should preach and I have always tried to imitate this. This sophisticated man of the world was first and foremost a seeker of God. He spent hours pushing wheelbarrows of manure to nourish the gardens and plants around the monastery. He acquired two nicknames in sign language. Manure Priest and Flower Priest. I guess it depended on whether or not you liked him as to which you used.

One day after confession he told me he was seeing a young lady for spiritual direction and that she wrote the most bizarre stories. He wasn't sure how he felt about her work. He let me read one of her short stories. Her name was Flannery O'Connnor. At that time, I had no idea who Flannery O'Connor was, but I soon found out and began to devour her books.

One day she was in the Gatehouse doing some shopping while walking on crutches. I went over to tell her I had just finished reading *The Violent Bear It Away* and had enjoyed it immensely, but I wasn't sure I had understood all of the symbolism. She laughed and said, "That's the only kind of criticism I trust. I'm always reading articles by literary critics analyzing what I meant and I don't have any idea what they are talking about!" She was always simple and straightforward, sometimes a little acerbic.

Apparently Father Paul occasionally went to Milledgeville to visit Flannery and her mother, Regina. While writing this, I checked *The Habit of Being* and found nine references to Father Paul and several references to his visits. If I had known about that, I would have pleaded to go along with him. Even though Flannery visited the monastery frequently, for spiritual direction, I only met her a few times by accident.

Father Paul never approved of my artwork. I was carving some Stations of the Cross for the cloister of the new building. They were self-conscious and modern (he called them modernistic). Actually, I was trying to get in synch with the gifted Otis and his helper, Bede, who were designing stained-glass windows. I thought realism was not the way to go, but did not really understand why. Otis had made a very modern stained-glass window for the new Church that depicted Our Lady and the Christ Child, and all of Bede's art was far out. You can detect here a kind of rivalry (on my part, anyway) that was not very spiritual. Neither Otis nor Bede ever commented on my artwork.

Father Paul's Church History classes were broadening my horizons, but I felt that my fervor for prayer and work was fading away. I was growing up also. Certainly my concept of monastic life had dropped back into this world. It was not ethereal, detached and other-worldly as I had dreamed. However, my longing for the priesthood had grown stronger. Looking to the day of ordination kept me going and I thought I would surely be more spiritual (holy!) when the holy oils had been smeared on my hands.

Father Paul also taught Scripture. The whole idea of "context" and "literary genres" was a revelation to me. Paul brought to life each book of the Bible and, more and more, I realized that my literal reading of the Bible had often missed the meaning. Many of the texts I had used to defend Catholic teachings against my high school Protestant friends were taken out of context and did not mean what I had tried to make them mean (with help of old-time Catholic polemical writers).

All of my education in the past had been fundamentalist, very conservative Catholicism. I had thought that Jesus founded the Church and made Peter the Pope and the Apostles Bishops; it was all passed down to us from that day to this day without change. Church History and Scripture disillusioned me of that kind of thinking. For the first time, I saw the complexities of it all. I really was losing what was an infantile faith. It was a painful process. At times, I thought I was losing my faith altogether.

Education in Casebook Morality

Father Augustine taught moral theology. He was a former Diocesan priest from Louisville and he had a lot of good stories and examples. Moral Theology was taught from the Latin text of Noldin which would be considered obsolete and very crude today, if there are any copies of it left.

The Noldin text always used examples of Bertha and Titsius, what they did (or committed) and "Quid Dicendum" ("what is to be said" about this case). It seemed ridiculous to me that they didn't teach us basic principles of morality and let us use our common sense. It seemed they wanted to spell out the moral right and wrong of every situation you could possibly think up. Imagine that. It reminded me of the Scribes and Pharisees of old.

As we completed De Sexto (*Concerning Sex*), Father Augustine let each of us write up a case and submit it to the class to be analyzed. You would be shocked at some of the cases. I thought, *So this is what these monks think about in their quiet time!* I thought it sounded like "delectatio morosa" (morbid delight), which was supposed to be sinful, but we were engaged in the scientific study of morality and so it was okay, our professor assured us. My personal contemplation of the subject carried over into the wee hours of the night!

These classes only deepened my personal sense of guilt and unworthiness, but I was determined to struggle for perfect chastity despite it all. God's grace would prevail, I thought.

Canon Law was the only subject that I got absolutely nothing from. I don't remember a thing from it, not even who taught it. This was deliberate! I still think it is a total waste of time and paper. Hebrew and Greek were interesting, fun and challenging. We did not have enough of either, only enough to read a very little bit and then forget it all, except for individual words.

Personal Crisis During the Time of Formation

In the middle of this very transitional time for me, something terrible happened. One morning after Matins, Brother Alanus (the procurator) came to the door of the Chapel and made a sign for me to come out, then made the sign "telephone." I knew this was an emergency because of the time (3 A.M.) and because we usually did not use the phone. I thought something had happened to my younger sister, whom I often worried about.

When I got to the office and picked up the phone, I heard my brother, Frank, say, "Bill, I have bad news for you. Mother just died at St. Thomas Hospital."

Mother had not been sick. She had been to see me two months before. I couldn't speak, didn't know what to say, so I mumbled things like, "What happened? Who was with her?" and then hung up. I was in a daze as I went out into the hall. The Abbot's office was right there, so I knocked. "My mother just died, Reverend Father."

He said, "Son, I'm terribly sorry. I will ask the monks to pray for you and your family." The Abbot was talking with another monk (who did not offer to leave) so I left and roamed around the

Margaret Johnson Nolan, Father Gabriel's mother.

cloister, then went in a little chapel in the back where seculars attended Mass.

A priest at Mass was reading the gospel passage, "Whoever leaves mother or father, sister or brother for my sake . . ." I broke down sobbing. I had just put a letter to my mother in the Abbot's mailbox that very day; I went running to get it back before it was mailed. I did not want my family to receive it. It would only sadden them more.

That day I just went to class as usual and kept my hands over my face to keep my tears from showing. Then I went to work where I was helping to dig a ditch for steam pipes in the new building. The brother in charge of work saw me crying and asked me what was wrong. I signed to him that my mother had died. He looked very concerned and told me to go back to the monastery for the rest of the work period and to take it easy. That evening at Chapter, the Abbot announced that Frater Gabriel's mother had died and he asked for prayers for my family and me.

I knew when I entered the monastery that monks were never allowed to go home for any reason, but I did not expect my mother to die so soon. My Confessor was of little comfort or help. He didn't seem to know what to say to me. I spoke to him once, maybe twice, and that was it.

It is hard for me to write about this. A young, twenty-two-year-old man should be free to attend his mother's funeral and be with his brothers and sisters. When I look at this objectively, I recognize the cruel inhumanity of a rule devised years ago by someone in France with a perverted sense of spirituality. But being a young man who believed that such a sacrifice was part of his gift of self to God, I never even considered demanding that I go to the funeral.

I reasoned that my mother was a woman of great faith. She would have understood my inability to come to her funeral and would have wanted me to observe the rule. My mother was a strong woman and I wanted to be like her. I cried a lot and felt sorry for myself, but I never rebelled outright. I was heartbroken that she would not be present for my ordination, to which she had looked forward with pride. My mother was the most important person in my life—and now she was gone.

I dreamed of my mother, down on her knees scrubbing floors and then suddenly in a glorious blue gown looking stately and beautiful. This dream was an allegory of her life. She was a Cinderella. She had never known her own mother, who died of influenza shortly after she was born. Her stepmother had raised her. She had never been nurtured or cuddled and had worked hard from childhood. Somehow I always knew this. It explains my instinctive pity for her. Probably it was her example that led me to seek out a life of sacrifice and self-abnegation as the way to holiness.

The day my mother died, my life lost its context and its focus temporarily. I believe it was that day that my Trappist vocation and my stability began to wobble. I swallowed tears and went through the motions of the monastic day. The day of her funeral I pictured her being buried in the cold, dark earth. I felt darkness closing around me also. It was so hard to pray. I did not feel very spiritual.

For a while, the relationships with my fellow monks (the more human ones) were holding me together. Their kindness, respect, and real love for me was evident in their "signs," their notes, and even a hug or two. Unfortunately, what I really wanted was someone to hold me close and let my cry until I was exhausted. Of course, that was not possible, so it was done in bed at night. My relationship with God was intangible, if existent at all, in the midst of this terrible pain.

Nine months later my father died. I had never been close to him but somehow I found myself crying hysterically at his death. I was an orphan now. Time to grow up. It was hard to grow up when you were not expressing your feelings and were trying to spiritualize all of your needs for affection and comfort. Life did go on for

61

me. I would keep studying for the priesthood . . . and so I continue with my story.

Frater Bruno, my classmate who used to carry the autobiography of the Little Flower around, came home from the hospital in Council Bluffs where he had been sent for treatment after his nervous breakdown. He was a different man: outspoken and assertive. He sat next to me in Chapter and he would mumble criticism (which was hilarious) about what was going on. He also would throw back his large sleeves and make the sign, "Useless!" The signal the Abbot always gave for ending Chapter was "Tu Autem." That was the phrase Bruno often mumbled when he wanted Chapter to end.

One morning when he was especially agitated, he intoned in a loud clear voice, "Tu Autem."

All the monks automatically sang out "Domine miserere nobis," and stood.

The Abbot stomped his foot and told us to sit down. He demanded to know who did that. Bruno groaned and raised his hand. "See me in my office," the Abbot said and then added, "Tu Autem!"

Bruno became one of my best friends as I was recovering from my mother's death. He was so delightful and so often expressed my feelings exactly. We sat next to each other at meals and we made so many signs to each other that the Abbot separated us, moving Bruno directly across the refectory. That made it even easier for us to see each other and make signs. Since Bruno had previously had a "nervous breakdown" (he was actually diagnosed as manic-depressive), he would not be allowed to be ordained. Canon Law forbade it. It was hard for him to see his classmates approaching that day but he accepted it pretty well. I admired him greatly and loved him dearly.

Once again, the fact that we were sometimes treated like children and things could be so harsh did not unduly upset me. It was part of humility. There was something else going on here. Feelings were not to be followed, according to the *Usages* (and even according to my home training). I took it that expressing feelings was a sign of weakness and even could lead you into sin. Until I was in my mid-twenties the battle against feelings that were too human was still a basic part of my life.

The happy days of novitiate when I felt great consolation in prayer were long gone. My Spiritual Director counseled patience. He said I was trying too hard. I should relax and let the Holy Spirit take over, but that was difficult to do. I wanted some tangible sign that I was growing in grace and coming closer to God. In reality, I was hoping for some mystical phenomenon—but nothing seemed to be happening. The intellectual pursuits of theology, Scripture, and languages took up a lot of time. Looking forward to ordination to the priesthood became the center of my spiritual life. That was a very concrete goal.

In those days there was a kind of mystique surrounding the priesthood in itself. It was the perfect way to holiness. A priest was an image of Christ in a very special way. The private Mass was a time of intimacy with Christ, offering the sacrifice of Calvary each day and living the mystery you celebrated there.

Frater Otis, Frater Lester, Frater Denis, and I were all preparing for ordination to the priesthood and the days were passing quickly. I thought I was not worthy to be ordained because of my preoccupation with sexual fantasies. An elderly Benedictine, Abbot Francis from St. Leo Abbey, was giving us a community retreat. He said to me, "Frater do you get up at 2 A.M. every day? Do you work hard on the new building? Do you attend all the Divine Offices? Fast regularly and pray faithfully? Do you love our Lord?" To each question I answered yes. He then said, "You are faithful 99 percent of the time, leave the rest to God." That relieved me and from that moment I was not tempted to turn back. I was ready to be ordained a priest soon.

Dom Robert was a real father to me, the only father I ever really had. He could read my moods. He truly loved us all and we knew it. He often told me I needed more "steel" in my character. He encouraged me to develop my talents. He took an interest in my art work and asked me to carve a wooden pectoral cross for him (the cross an Abbot wears as a sign of his Office). I carved a Gaelic Cross (he was Irish) with a dove on it representing the Holy Spirit (our monastery was Our Lady of Holy Spirit). He was buried with that cross around his neck.

A Great Revelation

The pineboard monastery was built in a quadrangle and housed almost one hundred members. This was something of a fire hazard. If a fire started while we were all asleep, it would not take long to consume the building and all of us. The Abbot instituted a "fire watch." Every night one monk would stay awake for three hours, followed by another monk who took over for the next four hours. During this shift he would go through all the buildings including the barns and the sawmill.

The Chapel was dark except for the little red lamp before the Blessed Sacrament. You could hear the ungodly screams of the peacocks that Flannery had given us. The Chapel made noises of cracking and popping occasionally but it was peaceful, not scary. It was a perfect time and place to drink in the silence and rest in God's presence.

What I did not enjoy was making the outside rounds. We had to go down a back road to the sawmill and pig and chicken houses. That could be eerie and each time I walked down to the cow barn and saw the silo where Brother Octavius had died, I hastened my step and almost ran back to the warm safety of the Chapel.

One way to pass the time on these watches was to go to the library, a room that was locked all week and open only on Sundays and Holy Days. But here in the middle of the night I had the keys to this room all to myself. One night I was in there looking around;

there were rows of books up high all around the top shelves that were turned around backward, with only the pages visible. The sides with the titles were to the back. Father Charles explained to me one day in signs that the top rows were "hell" (the signs for "fire" and "down"). That meant they were too secular and perhaps would be a temptation for monks and a time-wasting distraction. He did not approve of this "crazy arrangement" at all.

One night I climbed up there and began to investigate what was in "hell." I saw things like *Lady Chatterley's Lover* and *Anna Karenina.* You may be wondering why were they there at all? Well, people had a way of leaving their personal libraries to monasteries, so we had a little bit of everything. I guess that's why it was locked at all times. One night I found and began reading *Brothers Karamazov* by Dostoyevsky. I could not stop. I was on the first watch that night but I did not bother to wake up the person for the next watch. I kept reading and almost forgot to ring the bell at 2 A.M.

Naturally, I was most attracted to Aloysha and Father Zossima. In one passage where Father Zossima was outside the monastery hearing the sins of the peasants in the neighborhood, he listened to confessions of murder, adultery, cruelty, thievery and perversion with complete calm and quietly spoke words of forgiveness to each one, telling them only of God's love and mercy. I was so overwhelmed that I started to cry uncontrollably. I felt a shattering love for all human beings. I felt one with every suffering person on earth in that moment.

Father Zossima's spirit opened a new world for me. According to him, doing the "work of love" is everything. If you do that, you don't have to worry about faith. His love for Mitcha and his respect for Ivan's problems with faith showed me something of what God's love is like. My self-righteousness was torn out.

Father Zossima told Aloysha to return to the world; he could be a better monk there. When Father Zossima died, his body began to decay right away. The people thought his body should be preserved intact if he were truly a saint. His death did not fit the expectations of the pious for what a saint should be like. But Father Zossima was a human being like everyone else. My feelings about people, love, Christ, and holiness were revolutionized after meeting with Father Zossima.

I wanted to experience closeness to people and do the works of love that Aloysha had gone to do. He left the monastery and immersed himself in the world. This was a major turning point in my life. It changed my perception of the gospel, of human life, and of what it meant to follow Christ.

An Interlude of Disharmony: (Chant Wars)

Father Benedict was the choirmaster. He taught classes in Gregorian Chant to the monks once a week or so at the morning Chapter. He taught us that the Chant did not have a downbeat like modern music. You should lift your voice on the accents, and there were no measures or beats or time signs; the melody followed the words and enhanced them.

With only four lines and large square notes, this was all quite alien to the average American. The sound was ethereal, light, and very peaceful when chanted by a group of men (or women). Father Benedict had been to Solemnes (a Benedictine Abbey in France that is famous for its chant) to study the technique and fine points of Gregorian Chant. When he taught us the Chant at morning Chapter, it irritated some monks who did not like Gregorian Chant. They disliked the flamboyance with which Father Benedict would wave his arms all over the place while directing the choir. He would be all in a sweat when the class was over. These classes were a real penance for me.

Once there was actually a chant battle in the Chapel. Those who resisted Father Benedict were singing exactly opposite of what he taught and speeding up the words, which threw everyone into confusion. That was a shock to my system. Sacrilegious! Father Benedict and his opponents were reconciled after a few weeks, and the Chant calmed down.

Father Benedict became the Novice Master when Father Mary was promoted to Sub-Prior. Benedict was a workhorse. He threw himself into everything, especially into the work on the building where he was in charge of the concrete finishers. I was one of those concrete finishers. I became very fond of him. He was a big man (over six feet), clumsy, red-faced, thick glasses, and hair that receded, leaving a triangle of hair over his forehead. He poured sweat when he worked. One day he stepped backward and fell thirty feet off a scaffold, yet was back at work the next day. He was full of zeal but sometimes oblivious of common sense.

One of his novices was going to the urologist in Atlanta to be circumcised. He and Benedict rode the Greyhound bus into town to Dr. Coleman's office. The young man was all numbed and bandaged up after the surgery. They rode the bus back and both of them were in choir for Vespers. The anesthesia had worn off. The young novice courageously held onto the back of his stall in choir, barely able to bow.

The Infirmarian, Father Bernard, saw what was happening and wrote a note to the Abbot that the novice, Frater John, should be in the infirmary. The Abbot nodded yes vigorously. Bernard went over to take him upstairs but the boy could barely walk. They stopped every four feet or so, finally making it out of the Church. The rest of the brethren were distracted from their prayers. That's the Trappist way of doing things. Despite all the pain you just keep going until you can't. Benedict would have been rugged enough for it, but this poor child was not!

Although we were enlightened and educated twentieth-century monks, there was still the old Gethsemani attitude that the harder and more painful things were, the more you could endure, the better. Suffering was a gift and should be welcomed rather than avoided. I saw monks work until they almost passed out, pushing themselves when they were desperately ill, fasting when it wasn't necessary. I never liked pain and I avoided it in every way possible. *Another sign of weakness,* I thought.

As the spiritual books warned, you were supposed to treat all the brethren the same. I found that impossible to do. I liked a few people very much, couldn't stand a few others, but was congenial with most. I found ways to engage certain people whom I liked a lot in long sign conversations and I became very attached to them.

It was cold in the monastery during the wintertime. The Scriptorium was supposed to be heated, but it was still cold. I used to sneak over to the Guesthouse refectory (where it was warm) to study there. Brother Joseph (the Gatehouse brother who had carried my bags the day I came to the monastery as a recruit) was often in the secular dining-room setting the table or cleaning up. Although I was supposed to be studying Philosophy, it was more fun to make signs with Brother Joseph. He was charming and funny.

He often confided in me and told me (by signs) how hard the life was for him, and I told him how hard it was for me. He was often lonely and depressed, and having real trouble with celibacy. I shared those feelings and we often communicated about them. In the midst of one sign conversation, I mentioned to him how I hated the dry bread and barley water for breakfast (at 4:30 A.M.). He agreed it was pretty bad. I had forgotten about that until the next morning at breakfast when I found three pieces of raisin bread, some real butter, and a hot cup of real coffee.

Brother Joseph had access to such goodies from the Guesthouse. From that time on, I found these treats at my place frequently. We developed a fine relationship as the months went by, but I could tell that Brother Joseph was more and more troubled. My dear friend eventually left and went back to Arkansas, whence he came. He was a bright spot in my life on many cold winter days. I was very sad when he left us.

Sex and the Single Monk

The word monk means "one who is alone." A monk is one who has given himself wholly and completely to God. This total gift of self excludes giving oneself to any other person in the intimacy of a sexual relationship. This ideal was clear to me and I wanted to be faithful to God in the daily total giving of self to Him. But I was still a human being with a sexual drive and that caused real problems.

In our formation as monks, there was almost no discussion of sexuality. I remember some passages in spiritual books about sublimating these basic needs but I don't remember ever having open discussions on the subject. How can you love others intensely and realistically without wanting to show affection for them physically? "You can do that without becoming sexual," was the stock reply to that question. Even though we were all men, we never even touched each other in a friendly way. We were not encouraged to develop deep attachments to others in any way, but to love everyone supernaturally. We were never allowed to be in a room alone with another monk.

All of this made me one conflicted and confused young man despite all of the lofty ideals I professed. My teenage years had been a marathon of guilt and self-recrimination over sexual matters. The marathon continued in this holy place, but I fought valiantly for chastity. In my early Catholic education, they let us know about sins of the flesh without being too explicit. We got the clear message that all sex outside marriage was sinful. My higher education in the monastery did not broaden my understanding of sexuality in any way. Moral theology reinforced the fact that any form of sexual activity was gravely sinful for an unmarried person. That included masturbation. It also included deliberate dwelling on sexual thoughts. And in a Catholic teenager that meant forebodings of hell!

On one occasion Dom Eugene Boylan, the author of *This*

Tremendous Lover, told us during a retreat, "If you have never been in love, leave the monastery, fall in love, and then come back. Then you will know how to love God." I did not take his advice. In fact, I was shocked by it! But I thought about it a lot. I fantasized about being married, having a family and all the rest.

My personal confusion about sex and love were intensified by the fact that I had had an unfortunate sexual encounter at a very early age. A young high school student who lived across the street introduced me to some sexual activities one winter afternoon. He made me promise never to tell anyone about this. I was a child of seven years old at the time, preparing for my First Communion. I was preparing to receive Jesus into my heart. I knew my "house" should be all clean and ready for this Divine Guest! But my heart was sick when the time came because I realized I was in sin.

I didn't know how to tell anyone. I didn't know how to confess it, but I was sure I would go to hell because of it. About that time I saw a billboard warning about venereal disease. I asked my father what that meant. He explained that sometimes people contracted a fatal disease through sexual contact. From that point on I was sure that I had contracted a fatal disease but prayed that I would not die before being forgiven.

I prayed that when I got older or went to the seminary I would find a priest to help me out by absolving me from my sin. Meanwhile, I went on receiving Holy Communion in the state of sin which was considered a sacrilege.

During my eighth-grade year at school, a missionary priest gave us a retreat. One day he said, "I know some of you girls and boys may have done things that you thought were sinful but you didn't know how to talk about them. When you come to confession today, if you have a problem like that, just say, 'Father, I'm stuck,' and I'll help you."

I stood in line shaking and thinking of leaving but finally it was my turn. "Father, I'm stuck."

"Son, does this have something to do with sex?"

This is a photograph of Frater Gabriel as a child.

"Yes, Father."

"Alone or with others?"

"With others."

"Boy or girl?"

"Boy."

"Okay, son, you have gotten it out. From now on, don't ever be afraid to confess your sins. The priest is human, just as you are. We all need God's mercy and love. Just say a personal act of thanks to God for your penance, go in peace, do the best you can, and say a prayer for me sometime." I left in tears, full of joy, relief, and gratitude. I danced all the way home.

When I got home, there were cars everywhere on my street. I went in. The house was full of people. I went and sat down on the couch beside my mother. She said quietly, "Honey, your brother Gene is dead. We just got word from the Army officials." I hugged her, got up and wandered around the house in a daze, not speaking to anyone, aware of people touching me or patting me on the head.

In my mixed-up little head I thought maybe Gene, the perfect man who was now in heaven, had sent me the grace of Confession on the day of his death. I could become a priest now. This became the main focus of my life from that point on. But the preoccupation with sexual thoughts also continued. I felt sure the monastery would be a safe haven from all of this and that sex would be out of my life forever!

All of the above contained the makings of a real neurosis, and lots of tears and anxiety. It would have taken years of psychotherapy to unravel all of this! This tangled web of feelings and events could well have sent me to a mental institution. Instead it led me to a monastery. Thank God!

You may think that sounds strange but let me explain. The monastery did not educate me about sex at all. I had been traumatized in that area and I am not sure education would have helped anyway. My chances were slim of developing a normal sexual life as an adult. But in the monastery I lived with people who communicated care and concern. I learned to trust the goodness of others and to be genuine with them. It was safe to be with them. This made some emotional maturing possible for me.

I have always longed to love and be loved. I have engaged in all sorts of maneuvers in search of love and acceptance. I finally realized that I had this all along in my monastic family. It took me a while to understand and recognize that, mainly after I left.

People loving each other could be called the urge to give and to receive life. The older I grow the more I feel that need. For me it is the sole purpose of life. I have to find my own unique way to do that. Life is a mystery, always bigger than we are. It always keeps us seeking, finding our own way to love. As a monk, I did my best (and I still do) to give and receive life. I try to direct all my energy to this one purpose. Yet it is a struggle still and sometimes it seems impossible. I have never figured it out. How can you be in love with God and deal with the physical needs of your body at the same time?

No amount of praying eliminated the problems I had with chastity. I am sure others had similar difficulties, but any overt sexual activity that became known to superiors led to immediate expulsion from the community. I was painfully aware of this happening only once. I felt very sorry for the two people involved. In reality, I thought it was heartless when they were abruptly sent away and their names were never mentioned again. But that's the way it was. There was no tolerance for such behavior in the life we lived. Today such an event would be dealt with more compassionately, the guilty parties would have been given guidance, helped to a deeper insight and directed to another vocation, if appropriate. But not so in those days! Silence reigned here.

The Great Commandment

Every Saturday night we had a special service that symbolized fraternal charity. Two monks who were beginning their week as servants of the refectory and two monks who were finishing their week would don clean white aprons, take a bowl and pitcher, kneel before each professed monk, wash his feet and kiss them while the community sang Latin antiphons having to do with fraternal charity. This ceremony was called the "mandatum" (commandment) because Jesus had told his disciples to do what he had done at the Last Supper and wash each other's feet. In the Middle Ages this was considered a sacrament. We still did it once a week on Saturday evenings as a devotion. It was a reminder to us to serve each other and to put up with the faults of our brothers.

In preparation for the mandatum, we all washed our feet in buckets of hot water and lye soap after work on Saturday afternoon. This in itself was an act of charity! We put on clean monastic socks (made of coarse canvas-like material). Frater Otis had a clean pair on the bench beside him and when I started to sit down, my robe brushed his socks off the bench and into the water. He jumped up signing, "Look what you did. Look! Look!" He was extremely agitated. While I was beating my breast in contrition, he got madder and madder. I cracked up laughing. I couldn't help it. By this time all the other novices, sitting with their feet in buckets of water, were also laughing. I was afraid Otis would have a stroke. He never forgot that event. Even after all these years, he still mentions it occasionally when I see him. "How good it is for brothers to live in peace and unity."

Spiritual Growth and God

On Sunday afternoons I used to sit alone, for hours on the concrete wall that encircled the cemetery, with a book in my lap, feeling surrounded by the security of my monastic home. The two or three white concrete crosses with only a name on each were plain and stark. Someday a cross like this would say, "Father Mary Gabriel, O.C.S.O." That, too, was a comfort, I loved the clear blue skies of autumn and the cool breezes flapping my hood around. The fall of the year reminded me of the tale of my own life and it sort of made me long for that time when I would be old and ready to see what was beyond all this.

I thought of Father Ephrem, "drawn to God like steel to a magnet." He used to say, "Pray for my perseverance, not up to the end but *into* the end." That was my prayer too as I sat and prayed for perseverance. That did not mean just waiting for death but it meant to keep believing, to keep searching for God. I had not found Him yet; the search was for the whole of life.

The question that was stuck in my mind was, "Is there a God?" I had never been knocked off a horse and spoken with Christ. All my information was second-hand. Is this just a symbol for Ultimate Goodness, Beauty, Oneness, and Truth? My communication with God was always one way. I talked to God all the time honestly, desperately, but all I got back was an occasional insight, sometimes a little feeling of warmth, but mostly just silence. It was like God had already said everything He was going to say to us and now He would keep quiet until the end of time. But I still hoped for something: a small vision or an audible word or two, not a burning bush, just something that would let me know He was on the other end and that He even existed!

Other people talked about God like they had just seen Him in the other room. They knew exactly what He thought, what He wanted. For example, Dom James, the Abbot of Gethsemani, talked about Jesus like He was his "best buddy." He never seemed to have a doubt. Or the Spiritual Director who said to me, "You aren't listening." "Are you trying to tell God what to do?" "Don't you believe the Word of God?" He acted surprised that I had doubts about all this. Little did he know that I also had doubts about his calm certitude that it was all true. The only thing I knew was that I had not given up searching. There was a need that I couldn't be rid of, nothing had erased it. It was still there.

IV

Vespers: After the Work Day
Is Completed

Vespers is the late afternoon prayer after the work day is over. It is a warm and restful prayer often with a beautiful hymn celebrating the season of the year.

My studies were almost over. The time for that great, unimaginable day of ordination was coming. That was all I thought about. I kept a little journal with prayers and thoughts preparing for the pinnacle of my life. Years later when I discovered this journal I was embarrassed by the sentimentality of it and destroyed it.

The priesthood meant for me union with Christ. It meant to offer Christ present in the Eucharistic elements, to join myself with Him in offering the "Sacrifice of Calvary" each day, offering His perfect prayer for the whole of mankind. I looked forward to saying the words of consecration, and holding the Body and Blood of Jesus in my hands, holding Him up before the Father in an act of perfect adoration. That's what the role of the priest was. To me, the small silent cubicle of a side altar at 4 A.M. with only one person attending was the perfect setting for this sublime mystical action. I could understand why Father Ephrem often wept when he held up the Sacred Host and I could not wait to do the same.

You are ordained and become a priest when the Bishop lays his hands on your head without any words at all. It is the silent transmittal of the authority of the priesthood that has been passed down through the centuries, from Christ and the apostles to us.

When the day came, I don't remember those hands pressing down on my head. The whole ceremony is a blur to me. I do remember the Bishop smearing sweet-smelling oil on my palms then placing them together, wrapping them in a long bandage-like cloth and tying it. The cloth had been embroidered with my name and the date of my ordination by my nun sister, Sister Mary Bernadelle, RSM, whom I loved so much and who was ecstatic with joy over my ordination. Behind the altar the bandage was removed and a monk cleaned off my hands with lemon juice. There was a strong fragrant smell on my hands for the rest of the day.

All my brothers and sisters, a few cousins, and aunts and uncles attended the service. Afterward we had a big dinner over in the unfinished refectory of the new building. Otis, Denis, Lester, and I were ordained together—and all of the members of their families were also there together. Everyone was calling us "Father" and asking for our blessing. I found all of this excitement more than I could bear and was glad when the bell rang for Vespers. I felt like an imposter as I blessed people and they kissed my hands, yet I knew it was all true.

That evening after Compline I went downstairs to the kitchen where a young lay brother named Christopher was cleaning up. He had not been able to come to the ordination because he was cooking for all those people. He knelt down when I walked in and he signed, "Your blessing." I blessed him, he kissed my hands, and then I surprised myself by leaning over and hugging him tightly. He hugged back and I saw tears running down his cheeks. I knew that he was my brother indeed. That was another sacred moment on my ordination day. The thought of my mother was with me all that day.

Father Gabriel giving his first blessing to a visitor.

Death of a Giant

After ordination things went on as usual. Still a year of classes called Pastoral Theology which consisted of listening to Father Nicolas' often-repeated stories of his days as a secular priest. Manual labor now was making and finishing beds for the new building. But there was the new joy of offering Mass each day in the quiet morning hours. That made everything different even though it was the same regime of 2 A.M. rising, Divine Office, study, manual labor and poor meals and long periods of fasting.

One of the joys of being a new priest was hearing confessions. My first experience in this role was with a young lay brother called Moses. He was the kind of person that required little direction, and it was a pleasure to listen to him. For a twenty-year-old, he had remarkably good judgment. He was always the same, always positive. He had a great sense of humor and real compassion for others.

One day in spiritual direction (not confession), I asked him how he developed such an even disposition. I was thinking he must have come from a good home. Moses told me that he was born and raised in one of the worst slums in New York City. His parents were immigrants from Puerto Rico. They never went to Church and would not allow their kids to go. At eight or nine, he used to sneak out to go to Mass. When he was caught (waking up his father by accident), he was beaten brutally. He kept doing it and sometimes he got to Mass; sometimes he got a beating. He was often hungry and used to break off pieces of peeling paint next to his bed because it had a kind of sweet taste. Eventually, he became critically ill from doing this.

After hospitalization, Human Services took him into custody and sent him to a camp on Long Island. There he met a lady social worker who took him under her care. They developed a deep, lasting relationship. Even after he went home, they kept in touch. He said this experience transformed his life. He had tasted the joy of beauty and goodness, of giving and receiving love which he had always longed for but never had. He became more religious as he got older and in his teens landed at Conyers. He loved the life and all the monks were fond of him. He was one of the cooks and reveled in making the community happy by thinking up nice things to serve. The red beans and rice on Wednesdays were his specialty. It would be hard not to like this exuberant little fellow.

One day he got me for a session and I knew he was troubled. He was hesitant to get to the point. He was thinking of leaving the monastery. He was in simple vows (the three-year period of commitment) and he felt it would be wrong for him to leave. I asked him why he wanted to leave. He said he loved the monastic life and the monks were his family, but he wanted to be married and have a family of his own. He wanted to give his children the loving home he had never experienced. He had tears in his eyes. I felt like hugging him but did not. I told him that marriage would be a marvelous vocation for him and that maybe God was calling him to that vocation. He was surprised at my attitude. He perked up immediately and was all happy and smiling. He left a few months later, back to New York City. I don't know where he is today, but I'm certain he is a wonderful father and a good Catholic.

Right after ordination Father Otis was off to Gethsemani for a workshop of some sort. I knew he would be rubbing shoulders with Father Louis (Thomas Merton) and Father Raymond (also a famous author). I asked him to take some of my ordination cards and to get both of these "celebrity" monks to sign them for me. When Father Otis came home he handed me about six holy cards with elaborate messages from Father Raymond, "Congratulations, Gabriel, on your ordination to the Holy Priesthood. I hope you serve God with all your heart for many years, etc." Each card contained a different message, sounding as if he had known me all my life. Then Otis handed me one card, on the back of which was written in tiny script, "All honor and glory to God alone. Frater Mary Louis, O.C.S.O." That was the only contact I ever had with

Thomas Merton except standing beside him in choir once at Gethsemani. He sang very loudly.

The summer passed quickly. The Abbot, Dom Robert, was away at the General Chapter of the Order in Paris. One day in early October the Prior walked into Chapel during prayer and said, "Benedicite." We all responded, "Dominus." He said calmly, "Reverend Father just died of pneumonia in a hospital in Paris." That's all I remember. No feeling, no thought, no nothing. I didn't even cry. The next few days were a blank.

When the coffin arrived it was set in the Chapter Room of the new monastery. It was a European-made wooden coffin, sort of V-shaped, broad and octangular at the top, and narrow at the bottom. There was a small glass window through which you could see Dom Robert's face. The corners of his mouth were cracked, already decomposing. I thought about Father Zossima in the *Brothers Karamazov.* Dom Robert was not an "intact" saint either. He was too real for that! He would be buried in the crypt of the new Church. As the first Abbot of Conyers, he had built the new monastery and he had formed a generation of monks.

My real father, the only one I ever had, was gone. I knew that day that my whole life had changed again. Monastic life would never be the same for me. Later I found it was never to be the same for anyone under a new, younger Abbot and the coming of Vatican II. But it was Dom Robert who taught me to be a real monk by his wise words and his heroic kindness. I still love him for what he gave to me.

My grief over Dom Robert was buried deep down inside where grief over my mother still lay unexpressed. For me, deep feelings almost never saw the light of day. The monk who had nurtured me, given me self-respect, and loved me was gone.

Father Augustine Moore, who was a monk of Conyers, was a definitor (member of the Abbot General's Council in Rome). He flew back with the body of Dom Robert. After the funeral he was lodged in a room in the infirmary. He would stay home until after the election of a new Abbot. We all knew he would be a candidate for the office, along with several other outstanding monks such as Father Benedict (the workhorse), Father Joachim, the Prior, and one or two less likely candidates, including Father Paul Bourne.

Father Augustine had been a Confessor for the novices when I was a novice and Master of Scholastics when I was a student, so we had some history with each other—not all of it smooth. As Master of Scholastics, he was also Retreat Master in the Guest-house and professor of Dogmatic Theology. He was always gone somewhere and I felt he wasn't available enough to us, and thus the sometimes strained relationship with him. He was friendly, laid back, and a joy to be with when he was there. He was also loved and sought after by visitors in the Guesthouse and people from Atlanta. Despite his gregariousness, he knew how to keep his fellow monks at arm's length. He had been a hard worker as a monk. He planted rows of magnolia trees on each side of the drive leading up to the monastery. They are a landmark for the Conyers Monastery.

While I was visiting him, he mentioned that in the future monks would be sent to Rome to study and he thought that was a good idea. He noted that I might be a good candidate for such stud-ies. I wondered why he told me that.

All the professed monks are sequestered in the Chapter Room until they elect a new Abbot. Each monk casts his vote in secrecy. There are outside observers and counters, and this goes on until someone gets a majority of the votes. As expected, Joachim, Bene-dict, and Augustine received the most votes. Late in the afternoon Augustine finally emerged as the choice. The Father Immediate, Dom James, asked him to accept and after some humble words of reticence, he finally did accept. He would have to be confirmed by the Abbot General in Rome. Two monks went out to the Gatehouse to proclaim to the public the name of the newly elected. In Europe, there would be villagers out there waiting, but in

Conyers, Georgia it was only a formality. Our non-Catholic neighbors probably would not care one bit who had been elected.

The day of Father Augustine's blessing as Abbot was the coldest day in the history of Georgia. It was about ten degrees above zero and the holy water in the little dishes at the doors of the monks' cells was frozen solid.

All of us (professed monks and novices) boarded a Greyhound bus to go to the Cathedral of Christ the King in Atlanta for the ceremony. Of course, we all had nice clean habits for this public appearance. We had never been outside the enclosure as a group and this was most unusual.

There may have been a reception. I don't think the monks went. I think we celebrated back at the monastery. I was just relieved that it was all over. I broke out in a rash the next day from the stress. The dermatologist said, "Gabriel, you need to work out some of your problems."

I replied, "I've been trying all my life!"

A New Kind of Monastic Life

The Rule of St. Benedict provides for a "Father" for the community in the person of the Abbot. He is supposed to be a loving father, providing for each monk's needs and being concerned for each monk's spiritual well-being. His word is final in all things. His decisions are God's will (as long as they do not conflict with God's law).

Dom Robert had filled the role literally. There was no nonsense. We always knew who was in charge but we always knew we would be treated with understanding and compassion and that his decisions were made with our best interests at heart. Never did I doubt that.

The spirituality of Dom Robert was clear and simple. His strength and simplicity had created a certain security in the place. I felt he was a man after the heart of St. Benedict, a true contemplative, a searcher of God every day of his life. He had bequeathed that spirit to his monastic sons and I hoped I had absorbed it.

Dom Augustine was completely different in personality and in modus operandi, and it is not fair to compare him with Dom Robert. Augustine was more egalitarian. The first time I made a profound bow to him (the customary way of greeting Christ in the Abbot), he cracked up laughing and I responded, "But you really are the Abbot!" I saw a change in the whole dynamics of the community. We were more like a democracy. Augustine was the boss, the elder brother, but not at all a father figure. There was a new freedom in the air . . . a new permissiveness, I guess you would call it.

Parties became frequent: receptions for outsiders on anniversaries, Christmas, Easter, and so on. We were mixing a lot more with seculars, sharing our monastic life with them, showing "openness to the world." We were dispelling the myths of the mysterious monks who lived in total silence, except for saying "memento mori" (remember death) when they passed each other and who dug a shovel full of dirt from their grave each day. None of this was true but it was the image people had of Trappists and it needed to be eliminated, I guess. Trips to Atlanta were more frequent for anyone who had even the slightest reason for going.

In the old regime we had no television, radio, or newspapers. Now a TV was brought in for us to watch the Kennedy/Nixon debates because we were going to vote for the first time that year. Some adjustment of our sleep schedule had to be made for this. No one seemed to object to these new activities.

Monks began to be sent to Rome to study: Father Bernard who was Dean of Studies, Father Cyprian the Prior, Father Mary the Sub-Prior (who came home with the new name Joseph), Innocent the intellectual, and, of course without question, Father Otis. This stream of people being sent for higher education in Rome was really revolutionary. Besides all this the food was much better, but

Dom Augustine Moore, O.C.S.O., third Abbot of Conyers, who brought a new spirit of openness to monastic life in the community.

no meat yet. However, with trips to town more available, you could always have a steak while you were out.

Vatican II—A New Church

The Abbot had posted pictures on the bulletin board of the four or five Cardinals who were most likely to be elected Pope after the death of Pius XII. One of these men looked just like what I would have expected the degenerate Pope Alexander VI to look like. The day after the election, they took down all the pictures except the Alexander look-alike. That was John XXIII.

Pius the XII had been Pope since I was eight years old. He was an incredibly powerful spirit in a rather ethereal body. He looked holy and was always pictured in a prayerful pose or with arms outstretched embracing the world. He was called the Angelic Pastor. He had brought the Church to new heights of glory. He had also centralized Church authority very tightly under his hands and bishops throughout the world ruled in conformity with his mandates. External conformity was the visible hallmark of his reign. Catholics, triumphant in their own way, gave the impression of monolithic unity.

This explains to a large extent the kind of Catholicism I was raised in. The bishops in this country ruled their Dioceses (especially in the Northeast) like dictators. Their decrees were not to be questioned. They were political powers also. Priests and Sisters were trained in a very unbending and absolute way (and there were many of them). All wore uniforms and were taught to think alike, in conformity with orthodox Roman Catholic teachings and customs that extended far beyond the "deposit of faith" (the essential, defined beliefs of the Catholic Church). They, in turn, ruled their subjects autocratically. Most Catholics unthinkingly accepted many devotions, policies, and rules as part of defined faith which really were not such at all.

I was poured in that mold. It never occurred to me to question the Church. It would be unthinkable to question the holiness or the rightness of the Pope. He was venerated as the Representative of Christ on Earth. It never occurred to me that such religious formation bred immaturity and stifled creative thinking. These troubling thoughts would break forth in my mind a little later.

The new, elderly Pope John XXIII, who had been elected on October 28, 1958, would change the whole complexion of the Roman Catholic Church. This simple, earthy man of humility and good sense called a Council to "update" the Church. He "aired things out," and brought a sense of freedom, creativity, and honesty into every sphere of Church life. In reality a new day was here! There would never be such complete conformity in the Catholic Church again and there would be a new birth of scholarship and theological insight among God's people.

Vatican II not only let fresh air in but also let stale air out. With the stale air went a lot of tradition, practice, and piety. You would not think Trappist monasteries would have been affected too much by all of this, but they were. English in the liturgy posed a problem for Gregorian Chant that had developed around the Latin language. The large Psalters and Antiphonaries, which had been used for ages, were done away with. We read and chanted from notebooks a streamlined version of the Divine Office, drawn up by a committee.

The Trappists were regaining their monastic roots. We were all brothers in a family and the title "father" should be dropped. The mystique of the priesthood and the private Mass had developed around faulty theology and should not be encouraged anymore. The idea of prayer for the entire world, and penance and reparation for the sins of mankind took a backseat. Everyone should do his own praying. Period.

I had not read the primary sources for this new wave of monastic thinking, but all the intelligent monks were right on top of it and new ideas appeared at least once a month. If you clung to the old ways, God forbid! You were hopeless and just disregarded. A new day had arrived. Thomas Aquinas faded into the background along with Augustine and the Fathers of the Church. They weren't thrown out; they just were not mentioned much anymore. Theology was now being taught to students from contemporary authors and journal articles. Now I know that this was the end of Neo-Thomistic theology and the "know it all for certain" mentality to which I had been trained. I thought my world was falling apart and I resisted it for a long time.

I wondered when this enlightened theology would hit the sixth commandment. Was this the wave of new thinking that would set us free from all of the hang-ups about sex? Not exactly. The big word was "fundamental option." Apparently, if your fundamental option was for God it would require a complete change by an act of the will in order to commit a grave sin. This thinking made mortal sin rare for the average person who was trying to live well. This afforded a broader view of morality that was less a matter of rules and more one of the heart's orientation. That was, despite my insecurity, a welcome change from the biological moral theology I had been taught where physical details determined the degree of gravity for any sin.

Becoming a Teacher in a Uncertain Milieu

During this time of change, Dom Augustine assigned me to teaching Philosophy (when James, the current teacher, left for school). Then Scripture, then Monastic Formation, then Sociology, then anything that came up. I told him I was not qualified to teach at all. He said, "You read Latin well so that qualifies you for Philosophy. I'm sending you for training in Scripture soon and you can handle the rest." I did not agree.

At the same time, he even offered to send me to Rome to study. I declined the offer because I was confused at the time as to whether I would stay or leave. I did not want to be indebted to the community for further education if I did leave. He sent the brilliant young Innocent that year to study under Bernard Lonergan and Innocent never returned home but took a teaching job at Boston College when he arrived back in the States.

The whole Order was changing. The General Chapter and all the Abbots were exploring how monastic life fit into the "new Church." A lot was being written about more contemplation and less penitential athleticism. The only things I noticed were a little more sleep, less rigid rules, and better food. It was impossible to judge the quality of contemplation as to whether or not it had improved, unless they knew something I didn't know. Thomas Merton had influenced the attitude of the Order by his writing. He made a tremendous contribution toward more contemplative observances in Trappist monasteries.

Vatican II occasioned a new emphasis on Scripture study and there was a flood of new works on Scripture by outstanding scholars throughout the world.

Dom Augustine sent Father Fidelis and me to the Maryknoll house in Glen Ellen, Illinois, for a two-week workshop on Scripture, conducted by Father Barnabas Ahern, Roland Murphy, and David Stanley.

We were still under the old regime when it came to travel. Father Luke, the Wardrobe Keeper, packed bags for each of us with the essentials in it. He left a baggy black double-breasted suit, Roman collar, and Mennonite-looking hat for each of us to wear on the plane. The Abbot took us to the airport in the middle of the night. I had never been in an airplane and was uneasy. We got seated and noted the barf bags. Fidelis said, "You can have mine."

After we had been in the air hours longer than it should have taken to get to Chicago, I asked the flight attendant, who was wearing a St. Christopher medal, why it was taking so long. She stooped down to explain quietly that this was a prop jet and they had found that, when flown at full speed, vibrating endangered the wings, causing them to fall off several times. "Thanks," I gulped. "I understand." Fidelis reached for his barf bag.

When we got to our quarters at the Maryknoll house and unpacked, the only clothes we had were underwear, socks, and a wrinkled up robe and scapular. We were the only priests wearing a religious habit. All others had on sports clothes and teased us, telling us to relax and to get comfortable. But we didn't have any sports clothes to wear!

One evening several priests took us out to dinner (in our black Mennonite outfits). When drinks were ordered we did not know what to order (I didn't even know the name of a drink), so a priest ordered us, "Two martinis, straight up." A few sips of that thing and I could hardly walk over to the smorgasbord and back.

My dear sister, Bernie, a Mercy nun, was in Chicago at St. Xavier College. Visiting with her during that week was a bonus. She was so proud to have a brother as a Trappist priest. I was proud of her also. On one visit, the nuns at the college got our wrinkled habits and washed, pressed, and returned them smelling good and looking good. We must have stayed sequestered in a room while they did that because we didn't have any other clothes at the college.

The Scripture Workshop introduced me to a completely new understanding of Scripture. I found a stream of modern study that I loved and absorbed eagerly. There was nothing mediocre here! Barnabas Ahern, Rowland Murphy, and David Stanley were among the best scholars of the day.

When we got home, the Abbot asked us to update the library on Scripture. We gave him a long list of books that would be a good start in that direction. Most of the works we had on hand were ancient and outdated. The Abbot told us to go ahead and order the books. Many monks were delighted, especially Father Charles, the librarian.

V

Compline: The End of the Day

Compline is the night prayer thanking God for a fruitful day and asking for peaceful repose so that we may rise again refreshed and ready for another day of serving and praising our Creator.

This is a long way from where we started. I had come to the monastery in flight from the world and now I was becoming a man of the world absorbing all kinds of information and developing attitudes that I had never dreamed of before. I wanted to be open to the world in the spirit of John XXIII. My outlook had changed drastically in all ways. The sun was setting on my monastic vocation. My day of monastic life was almost over.

Dom Augustine was an enlightened superior. Under his patronage the library was always open. He also created a reading room with magazine racks for periodicals of all kinds, and I read avidly. It was now possible to keep informed on current events as well as current theology. Also TV was being brought in, and eventually was enthroned in one large conference room, supposedly to be watched only a few hours a week on Sunday afternoons.

I became quite interested in reading psychology. There were plenty of books now available by Karen Horney, Harry Stack Sullivan, Carl Jung, Sigmund Freud, and many others, enough to verify for me that I was a full-blown blossoming neurotic.

After harassing the Abbot to let me go for therapy for almost a year, he called me in one day to tell me he had met a young psychiatrist, Al Miller, who was a devout Catholic (that was essential!) and that he would be willing to see me free of charge. Later, I discovered that the offer was extended to several other monks. He started small groups of monks for therapy that we called "bunches" (in sign language).

My first day of psychotherapy I waited in a small empty room almost nose-to-nose with the receptionist, an elderly lady with white hair. An array of people walked through: a matronly looking lady carrying suitcases (a psychological examiner), an elderly doctor in a white coat, and a few people who looked like medical assistants of some sort. This office was located in a small white house on the grounds of a mental institution. I wondered if the doctor would declare me insane and commit me to the big white house on the hill.

When I finally got in, I was surprised to see a young man, not much older than I was, in a white coat. He was nice looking and he made me feel at ease right away. This was the beginning of a six- or seven-year relationship. Doctor Al Miller was not a devout Catholic in the traditional sense but he did have great respect for monastic life, as he understood it.

My first session was awkward because I wasn't sure why I was there, except that I felt screwed up. That was enough for Al. We started talking. When I left he wrote me a prescription for Librium twice a day. I was now in treatment. I didn't want the other monks to know this (they probably would have rejoiced at my good fortune), so I took my pills on the sly when no one was watching. Don't worry, I'm not going off on a history of my therapy! But, I do want to tell you a bit about Al Miller who was really part of our community for a good while.

Al Miller was not a saint. He used the usual profanities with complete abandon and with no apologies. He smoked cigarettes and enjoyed drinks with friends. He was a constant worker because he loved his work. His work was people, people who were lost and aching, people trying to find their way, people looking for help. He did not show these people where to go; he did not instruct. He just went with them wherever they went until finally they found a way that was good for them. Then he let them go.

He rushed a lot: to his car, down the highway, to a hospital, back to his office. He was always carrying papers, all disheveled, going to meetings. And I suspect the people he loved were always there in his heart, living inside him. He was warm to the touch, little beads of sweat on the top of his forehead near the hairline, tie loose around the neck, white crumpled shirt. I was amazed that he had time for me.

Al had thick lips and big blue eyes that were clear, looking steadily at you. He had unusually white teeth and his coal-black hair was always messed up. He put his feet up, leaned back and asked you what was going on and then soaked in your words. He patted you on the back when you left. He put his arm around you as he walked out of the office with you. He let you know you were great, asked you to write things for him, sculpt for him, tell him your secrets. He let you know he treasured all these gifts.

Al was a disciple of Harry Stack Sullivan. One of Sullivan's themes was, "We get sick in relationship, we can only get well in relationship." If our family relationships have been distorted we may never have known a healthy relationship. What did he mean by a healthy relationship! I found out in my sessions with him. He never used any psychological or psychiatric terms. He sincerely cared, in a down-to-earth, human way. Despite his M.D. and Ph.D. you never felt inferior in his presence. He told me once that in his work, above all the study and background knowledge, the one thing that counted most was that you really loved the people you worked with. I don't remember talking to him about my childhood sexual experiences. If I did, he did not put much emphasis on them.

He felt that a religious community should be a place where

people came to life, gave life to each other, and treasured the uniqueness of each person.

When I first went to see Al, my feelings had been denied or pushed out of my conscious life. When I felt myself becoming much attached to him, we talked about that. He said, "It's okay, don't worry." From that time on feelings began to pour out, feelings I had never been aware of. I used to be amazed at what came out of my mouth.

I was in awe of this man. I loved this man but I didn't know how to trust, how to give myself the way he did. He died before I learned that from him. He was still and cold and beautiful in the coffin, hair combed, shirt and tie immaculate. I stood and wept over him, all alone at 3 A.M. in the morning; no one else was there. I wished that I could breathe life into him as he had breathed life into me. We had not finished our work and now he was gone at such an early age. He was my primary teacher about realistic human love; I could go on because of him and try to love again and again.

Those years with Al and, of course, my love for Dom Robert, saved my life and made a human being out of me. But just as Dom Robert disappeared from my life suddenly, so did Al Miller. I cried a lot at his funeral. A few monks were there and Father Otis had composed a bland version of "Alleluia, The Strife Is O'er the Battle Done." My mother, Dom Robert, Al Miller—all the most important people in my life were gone now.

My relationship with each of them had been interrupted by sudden and unexpected death. There was no comfort in my aloneness. I was reading a little book at the time by Thomas Wolfe called *God's Lonely Man* where he seemed to say to me, "This is to be expected!" That is the price of loving. Wolfe's whole life had been a search for a father. I also knew what that meant. That was what my search for God was about.

The New Monastery

At long last the buildings that we had worked on for years and years were almost livable. The new Church would be blessed and we would move in soon.

Abbot Augustine decided we would have an open house before the new monastery was formally occupied and declared off limits to the outside world. He invited everyone to come and see our new home. It seemed half of Atlanta showed up.

The monks acted as guides for this occasion. We took small groups through all the regular places: dormitory, refectory, Scriptorium, and Church. We explained the Cistercian life to them along the way.

One of the groups I took was quite impressed. A man said, "This is amazing. These unworldly monks are so practical, so down to earth, honest, and normal. We never expected this!" I thought that was a great compliment to the community. But surely he's not talking about *me*. The day after the open house I broke out in a rash all over.

In the new building, I had been given a small private room in the snorers' dormitory. This was a place set aside for those who would otherwise disturb their neighbors while they were trying to get some sleep. I made it a cozy little area with a desk, books, and shelves that I had made of boards and concrete blocks.

On Christmas day, Father Charles knocked on my door. He had an entourage of younger monks behind him. He had a record player and an album of Judy Garland that someone had sent him for Christmas. He and these monks had come bearing cookies and Cokes for a Christmas party. I had been chosen as the host for this occasion. I let them in and the party began. As we listened to Judy sing, Father Charles gestured and made signs about how incredible Garland was and we all nodded in agreement as we ate cookies. I drank a Coke in resentful silence.

You may think that this little episode was quite harmless.

A view of the library wing of the new monastery during the final days of the construction.

What's wrong with a little celebration like that? Nothing. Monks are very real people who like good music and often have cookie crumbs on their scapulars—but it still seemed ridiculous for grown men to have to have a party like this secretly. Somehow the whole thing appeared incongruous. My disillusionment had to do with the fact that I had expected monastic life to be "different." I had wanted to be holy and I expected myself and everyone else to be seeking "one thing only." That was not exactly realistic on my part. This party sort of embodied that fact for me. Monks, including myself, were like everyone else!

In our newly built monastery we were much better organized. Father Bernard, Dean of Studies, had drawn up an excellent curriculum of studies for the monks in formation. Education for monks of the future was to be of higher quality. He had talked about making overtures to Emory University to arrange an extension for us so that we could issue degrees through them. Gabriel Marcel, the Christian existentialist, came out to speak to us while he was at Emory. He had a walrus mustache, and was short and round. I didn't understand a word of the French accent with which he spoke English. The only thing educational for me was that I now had seen in person, a man of such stature in the world of philosophy.

Years later when I applied to the University of Tennessee, the Admissions Office received as transcript from Conyers written in Latin. The Dean of Admissions called me over and said, "Would you send it back and have it translated into English?" I did so and enclosed a little note saying, "Make the English translation impressive." When the transcript was returned, the Dean of Admissions said, "You probably have enough material here for a Ph.D. but, unfortunately, your credits are not recognized by the State of Tennessee."

When Doctor Victor Frankl was visiting Emory for a convention of psychiatrists, he came to Conyers to speak to the community about Logo Therapy. Most of us were familiar with his work, *Man's Search for Meaning*. His talk was not so much didactic as it was a warm, personal dialogue about his own inner life. This was very moving. He was so grateful that he, a Jew, would be invited to speak to a group of Christian Trappist monks.

Toward the closing of his talk he took out a handful of pebbles and offered them as a gift to the community. He said, "These pebbles are from the Mount of Beatitudes. The very feet of Jesus may have touched them. They are a gift and symbol of our meeting here. May we be together in eternity." Then tears started to roll down his cheeks. He said, "I cannot talk this way to a group of psychiatrists. I must be more scientific with them, but you are my brothers and I can weep with you." Even now I choke up thinking of this loving, honest man.

The Call of the World

The innocent idealistic young monk I have been describing to you was becoming older, maybe wiser, and maybe a bit cynical. It was no longer the hardships of monastic life that were causing me to want to leave but now it was the "fleshpots of Egypt." I wanted the pleasures and enjoyments that people "out there" had. I wanted more autonomy, more freedom to be myself and do what I wanted to do. Total dedication to God alone sort of faded out. It was no longer uppermost in my mind. Lots of other things were.

Because of Vatican II, everyone was hoping for great things. I had felt it was all talk and I had heard it before. Nothing would really change. The bishops would get together and put the same teachings into more modern sounding words and that would be it. But as the Council continued and concluded it became clear to me that everything had changed drastically.

Al Miller, had prepared me for "re-entry" to the secular world of the 1960s, if that were possible!

The Abbot knew I was thinking of leaving. He appointed me Guest Master. That meant talking care of the Guesthouse and offering hospitality to all who came for visits to the monastery. This required trips to Conyers and to Atlanta to pick up guests who arrived at the airport. This put me more and more in contact with the secular world.

At the age of twenty-eight I was taught to drive by Brother Damian, a brave and patient soul. We eventually risked Atlanta traffic on the Interstate. The guests I picked up had no idea of the danger they were facing.

The first time I showed a group of men retreatments around the monastery, I eloquently expounded on how strict the life was because I knew that was what they wanted to hear. I showed them the austere refectory and the Scriptorium. When we came to the dormitory with the bare cells, I pulled back the curtain of one to show them the straw mattress and pillow on bare boards. One of the men asked, "Can we see the chastiser?" I had to stop and think. What was he talking about? Then it came to me. He meant the discipline with which we flogged ourselves on Friday mornings. I laughed and said, "Sure." I pulled back the pillow of this monk's bed where it was usually kept. There under the pillow were three King Edward cigars next to the discipline! They all laughed heartily.

One of them asked, "Are you allowed to smoke?"

I sighed, "No. That's contraband. I don't know where he got those, but it's against the rules."

By this time I felt spiritually bankrupt. My Confessor was Father Paul whom I mentioned in connection with Flannery O'Connor. In our hours of spiritual direction we often strayed into conversation about art, music, travel, and even a little gossip. Part of this, I think, was due to my inability to explain to him what my crisis was about. Maybe the foundation of my monastic life had been built on sand to begin with? The monastic cowl, the habit, the strict regime had been romanticized in my mind. I had wanted to "leave the world," live a life hidden in Christ, living the gospel literally with a family of men who also were doing the same thing. I must say that many of these men were doing all that quite faithfully—to my amazement. Many of them were struggling, I'm sure, just like I was. But I was disillusioned with myself and with monastic life. This environment in the Guesthouse was daily making me more comfortable with the ways of the world.

I began to feel that the life in the active ministry would be an exciting place to be. However, I had solemn vows and that presented a conscience problem. I had promised God that I would live as a monk until death. I spoke to dear Father Ephrem (then eighty-eight years old). He listened quietly and kindly. I was waiting for a rebuttal from him. He looked straight at me and said, "Dear boy, you love God very much and God loves you. If you feel you can serve Him better and that you would be happier as a secular priest, go in peace and share your love for God with the people you serve. You are not forsaking your vows, but living them differently." I embraced that dear holy man and cried on his shoulder for a while.

Also, I remembered a hand-written note that Bishop Adrian (a former Bishop of Nashville) sent to me on the occasion of my solemn vows. He congratulated me, assured me of his prayers and best wishes, and then added, "You will always be welcomed back with open arms if you ever come home to the Diocese of Nashville." That made me feel less guilty.

I was not sad at the thought of leaving my fellow monks. I was anxious to get out and start living a new life in the world outside. I had a rosy picture of creature comforts and good times. Maybe unconsciously I wanted to live some of the adventures I had missed in my late teens and early twenties.

Because of these preoccupations, my leaving behind seventeen years of monastic life was almost a mindless rush to "get out." I did not do a lot reflection on what I was doing or even spend any time praying about it. My mind was made up and, mentally, I was gone from there. I said goodbye to my closest friends (by signs), but I don't remember any tears or regrets. The Abbot gave me a last warning that I had lived away from the world for a long time and that the adjustment to a totally different environment would be chaotic. I didn't listen to him. I was eager to go. My heart was singing. I remember hearing over and over in my mind the song, "The Hills Are Alive with the Sound of Music!" I couldn't wait.

The Abbot let me go to Conyers, and buy some secular clothes, including sport shirts. This shopping trip and three hundred dollars cash was my parting gift as I prepared to leave after seventeen years in the monastery.

Now I know that some loss of trust came in the wake of everything changing so rapidly at the time of Vatican II. Everything I had been trained in since the age of eighteen was being discarded. Finally, I think I just gave up, let the past go, and convinced myself that I would be able to pursue a new set of ideals out in the world. I was preparing to do that with great hope.

Now, after living in the outside world for a while, what do I think of the life I left? I think the desire to live such a life of dedication and spirituality lies deep in most people—from Buddhist and Christian monks, Muslim mystics, Hindu holy men, to ordinary people. I am comforted that communities still live the contemplative life. It is also possible to live such a life "in the world." I believe the "blessed" people that Jesus spoke of (the poor, the humble, the merciful, and the peacemakers) are believers and unbelievers whether in monasteries or on the streets of cities and villages everywhere. I believe the pathos, the heartbreak, the joys of ordinary people are the domain of God's kingdom. That's found right where we are. That's the kingdom Jesus was talking about.

People sometimes ask me if I consider those seventeen years in the monastery a waste. That's not easy to answer. I do have a few regrets but overall I have to say no. In those years I grew up. They were years of searching and longing for God. What I learned there was priceless.

I went to the monastery seeking the secret of life's meaning. To some extent, I actually found it there. There were no visions or voices, no startling revelations. I found honesty, the hard facts of life, and respect for my brothers, the fragile human beings I have described here. I found the joy that sacrifice can bring when you care about other people. I learned not to demand from life what it does not have to give, not to demand from people (including myself) what they are not capable of giving. I learned that day in and day out sameness can offer peace, that people become more precious when you know them painfully beyond pretense and phoniness. I learned about honesty which is the only solid ground. I don't think that was all a waste. After that it was time for me to leave, to go outside and return to the world, and to seek a new life.

I've been leaving home since the age of eighteen and am still searching. The disappointments and losses of life have kept me looking forward with hope. My dreams and ideals have given way to a different reality than I first envisioned. Moving ahead and leaving behind the past is painful but I keep believing there is always "Something More."

This is the end of my recollections. I would like to leave you with some profound words of wisdom, but I don't want to be a phony at the end. Writing this has made me realize that finally, "Love is all there is." I have spent a lot of time and some pages here, moaning about not having much love in my life. But all of the stories you have read here, these human encounters, were about people doing the best they could to care. Remembering them has made me realize how much I was loved and how much I loved others without analyzing what was offered to me so many times. In the future, I want to treasure every moment of contact with fragile human beings because that's the only home I have. That's where God lives.

VI

The Salve Regina

The good night hymn to Our Lady is the last prayer of the day for the monks. They retire in trust that all is well in God's care.

My life was not over when I left the monastery. I wept during the Salve Regina on my last night there, just as I had on my first night there. I was leaving to face a chaotic world of 1966. That's another story.

Thanks for reading this. Godspeed on your journey!

Father William Nolan

(Father Mary Gabriel, O.C.S.O.)

A statue of Our Lady of Grace sculptured in clay to be cast in concrete for the façade of a school in Atlanta. The statue was carved by Father Gabriel, O.C.S.O.

The One O'Clock Jump

Oh, heavenly hash and glory stew
Such a holy hurly-burly.
When Angel Gabriel Junior blew
Reveille an hour early!

Chorus:
It's Gabriel this and it's Gabriel that
And it's, "HANG HIM ON A TREE!!"
But it's, "Lover of Humanity,"
When he gets us up at three!!

The sleepy saints crept down the stair
All dressed in shoe and sock.
There's nothing plural anywhere
It's only **one o'clock.**

Chorus:
It's Gabriel this and it's Gabriel that
And, "Pull his feathers out alive!!"
But it's, "Take a bow," and, "Tip your hat,"
When he pulls us out at five.

The cherubs howled, the angels cried,
And threw their halos at the sun.
The nine-fold choir heaved and sighed
"He's upped us up at one!!"

Chorus:
It's Gabriel this and it's Gabriel that
And, "Kick him out of heaven."
But it's, "Vivas in aeternum,"
When he rings the bell at seven.

106

When Heaven's Queen had heard the thing
She simply smiled and said,
"My children get up at one o'clock,
But I never go to bed."

Chorus:
It's Gabriel this and it's Gabriel that
And, "Go to the end of the line."
But it's, "Please to walk in front, Sir!"
When the alarm goes off at nine.

Jesus told His Father
And His Spirit, One in Three,
"We are up forever
From all eternity!"

Chorus:
It's Gabriel this and Gabriel that
And, "Send him to the moon!"
But it's, "Stay him up with flowers,"
When he lets us sleep 'til noon.

Finale:
Yes, at three o'clock, at daybreak
At seven, ten and noon—
Oh, wake us up or blow us up
Anything but too soon.

Composed by Father Bernard
Between 1:00 A.M. and 2:00 A.M.
December 3, 1953